the Entrepreneur's BIBLE

52 Proverbs of PROFIT

Rick Duree

LINDENWOOD UNIVERSITY PRESS

Kristi,

Generosity is underappreciated by the masses, but highly coveted by entrepreneurs. When you make your millions, remember the 4th Knuckle (Proverb 8). Great job,

[signature]

DEDICATION

To all the struggling entrepreneurs out there who need a partner, a mentor, an advocate to stand up and tell them their ideas have promise, and that they can do it, and to give them a swift kick in the rear when the time comes. To all who are ready for the challenge, this book is for you.

PRAISE FOR 52 PROVERBS OF PROFIT

"An easy read with lots of humor but still gets down to business!
Well done!"

- Jim Jump, Host of the show, "The Business Roundtable" on LUTV

"Rick Duree's plain spoken advice tells aspiring entrepreneurs
what the real world of entrepreneurship is like, and how to
navigate the mine fields on your path to success. A fun read with
lots of common sense lessons for everyone."

-David Rosenwasser, Former President, Promotion Management Inc.

"Read a chapter a week in order, or skip around – it does not
matter. This book will open your eyes to new possibilities."

- Steve Epner, Founder, Brown Smith Wallace Consulting

"Rick Duree is different from the many authors of books on
entrepreneurship—he's actually conceived, financed, and built
successful ventures from the ground up. He also writes in a very
entertaining and relatable fashion. It's a valuable and fun read."

- Ed Morris, Professor and Former Dean, Lindenwood University

"Truth is that which looks the same when viewed from all
perspectives. This is a book of truth."

- Lawrence R. Lund, C.F.P.

"A must-read for both seasoned and aspiring entrepreneurs. It's
smart, entertaining and, most importantly, spot on in its analysis
of what it takes to be a successful independent business person.
Huge bonus points for the awesome illustrations."

- Jan Christian Andersen, President, Ignition Tank

"Rick Duree's book is a compilation of "idea gems" for
entrepreneurs, he expresses simple truths with a generous dose
of wisdom from his real-world experience - everything a proverb
should be."

- Paul Heirendt, co-organizer, 1 Million Cups

ISBN: 978-0-9894421-3-8

Design by Zamudio Creative Group, St. Charles, MO
Illustrations by Alvin Zamudio and Sean Long

Printed in the United States of America
14 15 16 17 18   5 4 3 2 1

Contents

Entrepreneurial Marketing   125

Your business is your business. You share the successes with your team, but own the mistakes yourself.

Entrepreneurial Expansion

INTRODUCTION

 grew up in the outskirts of St. Louis. My home town had more churches than people. There were seven of us kids plus mom and dad all living in a 1,000 square foot home in the sticks. (I still remember how blessed/cursed we were with our single bathroom). Needless to say, with that many people living on top of one another, peace at home was at a premium.

The economists classified us as "working poor." I agreed with them. Dad worked three jobs. Mom worked part-time at the local Wal-Mart when it opened. We kids worked the fireworks stand in the summer and fast food at night after school when we got old enough. We did what we had to do to get by, as most people did. But I always told myself that those jobs were simply a means to an end. I had bigger dreams pulling on me night and day, and I knew that entrepreneurship was one of the ways to realize them.

I began my path following the normal steps the "experts" gave us all to get ahead. You know: get good grades, graduate high school, go to college, get a good job, and climb the corporate ladder to some kind of financial success and stability. OK, college was fun, I'll give ya that. But the corporate life didn't really appeal to me. So, I constantly kept my eyes open for any needs in the community,that weren't being satisfied by the market.

I first thought, "there are no good deals left to be had. Smart people have already solved all the obvious problems out there. I'll be lucky to find anything that really stands out. I'm gonna be stuck in this dead end job for the next forty years!" Depressing? You betcha. But once I fought past my mental block, I tried something that helped me find the so-called "pain" I could sooth out there in the market. It opened my eyes to possibilities I had no concept of previously. (Take note! This next thing may actually change your life.) I started my first "Idea Notebook." Every day I pushed myself to:

1. Find one product or service currently available in the market that I thought needed to be improved in some way.

2. Create one new product or service that didn't exist to my knowledge, but that I wanted to see offered.

All day long, I'd pay attention to anything I was buying, driving, eating, or using in any way, to see if I could find some masterful improvement just on the precipice of being developed. At the same time, I'd think about what products or services people needed that weren't out there in the world. The secret to creating new business solutions or product lines that people will love is discovering what people are doing inefficiently—the "pain" of wasted time, money, and manpower. If you keep your eyes open, think outside of your own experience, and question the logistics of the workings around you, you'll be surprised how many improvements and new creations come into your vision. You can both serve your fellow man by bringing these improvements to market, and earn a living for yourself and those you care about. It's that easy!

Ok, it's not easy per say, but it is that simple. Think about it. What does the word "Entrepreneurship" mean to you? What does it look like through your looking glass? Do you know it when you see it? Is the old school image of the light bulb the best symbol for it? Recently, I asked a few guys what their definition of entrepreneurship was. "Money! It's all about making money," one guy blurted out. "Yeah, money," the next guy said, "and change. You have to be able to change with the market."

These are pretty common answers that only comprise a small part of what entrepreneurship means to me. One day I had a brainstorming session with a buddy over some hot wings. I wanted his help developing a new image that could represent my vision of entrepreneurship. Here are many of the words that came to mind...

As you can see, entrepreneurship is HUGE! It's all-encompassing, housed in both the crafty, intuitive right side of the brain and the objective, logical left. When you're solving problems or creating something new your entrepreneurial skill set is constantly being tapped, from the trendy brand you strive so hard to build, to your functional web interface.

See if this next depiction fits you. Like many entrepreneurs, you crawl out of bed in the morning and jump in the shower just to find your thoughts wandering toward your calendar. Before you know it, you've planned out your whole day right down to who you'll be calling on the drive to and from work (not the safest past-time). As you arrive at work, you check your to-do list for the day's tasks, but keep your eyes open for other opportunities. Maybe you have lunch with some interesting people hoping to build up your professional network. You wonder how you might connect people and services in new and interesting ways. Invariably, things pop up to fill the afternoon, and the drive home phone calls mirror the morning commute. Even the evening is occasionally interrupted by whatever pressing business is at hand.

Let's be honest, sometimes you want a break from the creative thinking, the problem solving, the conversations. It can get to be too much. Soon enough you find yourself trying to turn your mind off, if just for a day. Good luck at that. We entrepreneurs tell ourselves that shutting down doesn't pay the bills or satisfy needy customers. Every minute we rest is another minute we're not selling. But even more than that, down to our core, stagnation simply doesn't feel right. We are the movers and shakers in our communities, making change happen right before our eyes. We're leading entrepreneurial lives...and we love it!

My buddy, an inspirational speaker and businessman who faced many personal obstacles on his road to entrepreneurial success, told me that as a kid he was diagnosed with ADD (Attention Deficit Disorder). He used to feel down a bit because of this label that had been put on him by the "professionals." Later in life, as he built his entrepreneurial empire, he noticed that many other entrepreneurs had symptoms of ADD, too. They would jump from project to project creating new widgets and innovative ways of doing things. They would build up an idea, put a team in place to operate it, and then jump to the next interesting endeavor, hoping all the while that what they built could stand on its own. They never stood still!

Some might call it multi-tasking, but his entrepreneurial friends never sat around long enough to finish anything they started, so my buddy labeled it "attention deficit" and threw his head back and laughed! He finally understood how ADD applied to him. He definitely had "attention deficit," but it wasn't a disorder at all. It was how he saw the world, created new industry, and dealt with problems. It was part of his journey, his Entrepreneurial Life, and he's been laughing all the way to the bank ever since.

Think about where you are right now and where you're going over the next two or three years. What are your

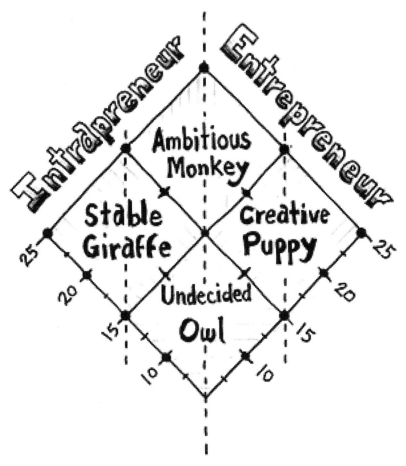

goals? Are any of your New Year's resolutions still in effect? How far along are you in actually reaching your dreams? Look at the graph below. Do a quick self evaluation and decide where you land on the Duree Diamond Entrepreneurship Personality Test.

NOTE: There are no right or wrong answers, no better or worse Animal Quadrant to land in. You are who you are. Your life experiences and choices have led you to make decisions in a unique and personal way. Those values will be reflected by your score on this short version of the Duree Diamond. (The long version of the Duree Diamond Entrepreneurship Personality Test will be in the upcoming book in my Entrepreneur's Bible Series under the title Genesis: Becoming an Entrepreneur. Check it out if you want to delve deeper and learn more about your entrepreneurial personality.)

DIRECTIONS:

Rank yourself 1 to 5 (5 being highest) on how much the following sentences reflect your personality. Once you've scored each sentence from SIDE 'A' as it relates to your personality, add up your total and move yourself up the left side of the Duree Diamond. Then score each sentence from SIDE 'B,' add up your total, and move yourself up that much on the right side of the graph. Your two scores will intersect within one of the Animal Quadrants of the Diamond. Take out a pencil and make a mark on the graph where you land. We'll look back on this again at the end of the book to see if you've moved within your Quadrant at all, or perhaps even jumped animals. I bet you'll be surprised where you end up after reading these 52 Proverbs of Profit.

QUESTIONS: Rank yourself 1 to 5 (5 being highest)

SIDE 'A':

_____ Stability is one of the most important focuses in your life.

_____ You actively avoid risk whenever possible.

_____ You live day-to-day, generally guided by very short term goals.

_____ You find success most often when you follow directions.

_____ You like having a structured daily routine.

_____ SIDE 'A' TOTAL

SIDE 'B':

_____ You're creative in most aspects of your life.

_____ You can tolerate higher levels of risk pretty well.

_____ Your friends think of you as a problem solver.

_____ You always have major long-term goals you're working toward.

_____ You're good at thinking outside the box.

_____ SIDE 'B' TOTAL

UNDERSTANDING THE QUADRANTS:

The Animal Quadrant you land in is largely representative of your entrepreneurial personality. However, the next closest Quadrant can also be instructive as you may possess a few of those traits, too. Think of this connection as having both a Major and a Minor in college. The Major is your focus, the Minor supplements your aptitudes.

If you land on or very near a line separating Animal Quadrants, you can go either way. You have traits from both animals as a hybrid would, taking on their strengths and weaknesses. You're a mule of sorts! Think of this as having two Majors in college. Both direct your efforts in life, reinforcing each other, often tempering assertiveness and aggression with caution and pragmatism.

ANIMALS:

Creative Puppy: You're a "Serial Entrepreneur" (see below for definition), ambitious, always solving problems, whether they're your problems to solve or not. The terms creative and innovative define you, as you can't help but think outside the box. Now for the Tough Talk – Like an excited Puppy, you have somewhat of an attention deficit (see Introduction), and find it difficult to complete projects. You're 80/20 like me (see Proverb 13). Welcome to the family!

Ambitious Monkey: Like a happy Monkey, you ambitiously climb ladders in business and the community. You're a great team member and problem solver going from project to project leading others as well as following directions. Now for the Tough Talk - You can see yourself taking a risk and becoming an entrepreneur, but because you have found success and excelled within an organization, the odds are less than 50/50 that you will choose to go out on your own and start a business.

Stable Giraffe: As a "Stability Rock" (see below for definition) you value structure in your day, follow directions like a pro, and work well within an organization. You look for jobs that provide benefits and flex time, but often live paycheck to paycheck. Now for the Tough Talk - Giraffes are cautious, tall, mighty, and swift, but if they stumble it's a long way down and difficult to get back up. Unfortunately, you are subject to management, with the threat of unemployment looming over your head.

Undecided Owl: Frankly, I'm impressed you took this personality test, seeing that you're so indecisive... (kidding). First, the Tough Talk: You're not sure what your future holds, so you find it difficult to set long-term goals and commit yourself in any one direction. You aren't going out of your way to be a leader right now, either living paycheck to paycheck, or going to school, and you may regularly benefit from the charity of others. Now, the Possibilities - If you don't like being an Owl sitting silently on a tree branch watching others play, the good news is you can grow into any Animal Quadrant you want! No matter what your age, the sky's the limit for Owls! If you can find direction and a greater purpose in your life than video games, you can morph into any of the other animals on the Duree Diamond. This book can help you, maybe more than anyone else. Read on and really apply the 52 Proverbs of Profit to your life. The future is bright.

INTRAPRENEUR vs ENTREPRENEUR:

If you land on the LEFT HALF of the Duree Diamond, you are more of an Intrapraneur, someone who, while working within an organization, actively solves problems throughout the division, and uses creative skills to develop new products or lines of business.

If you land on the RIGHT HALF of the Diamond, you are an Entrepreneur, trading risk for return, working within an organizational framework you developed to creatively solve problems and limit market inefficiencies.

STABILITY ROCK vs SERIAL ENTREPRENEUR:

If you find yourself landing on the FAR LEFT CORNER of the Duree Diamond, realize that you're probably not interested in trading risk for reward in the traditional definition. You find your niche thriving in a controlled and structured environment where you are safe to produce quality products and services within an organization. You and others like you are vital players in the economy, and coveted employees in Fortune 500 companies. Congratulations, you're a Stability Rock! Remember the old children's song "the Wise Man and the Foolish Man?" In that song the wise man built his house upon the rock, and the house didn't go out of business...or something like that. You are that rock!

If you find yourself landing on the FAR RIGHT COR-NER of the Duree Diamond, realize that you like taking chances. You find your niche constantly forging new ventures and riding them as far as your interest allows. You and others like you are the world's thinkers, building businesses that solve the most pressing problems of our day. Congratulations, you're a Serial Entrepreneur! Again, remember the old children's song "the Wise Man and the Foolish Man?" You are both the wise man and the foolish man. Sometimes your ideas get blown down and you have to go back to the drawing board (see Proverb 49). But because you're always thinking, eventually you're gonna have one with a firm foundation that'll stand the test of time.

CONCLUSION:

Are you happy with where you find yourself on the Duree Diamond? If not, is there passion inside to push on to the next level? No matter where you place yourself on the Diamond right now, these 52 Proverbs of Profit will help you reach the next level in your own unique Entrepreneurial Life. I know you can get to where you want to be no matter what obstacles stand in your way. We'll fight forward together. Entrepreneurship for all who desire it is my personal goal. If you're striving to reach that next level, read on.

Entrepreneurial
STARTUP

Proverb # 1

It's not about being in business, it's about staying in business!

hen I got my first bank loan, my banker asked, "are you ready for your first withdrawal?" I said, "sure!" To which he asked, "how much do you need?" I said, "$10,000? I think that sounds like a good number." (I was so professional back then!) He replied, "OK. Do you want to count it out with me to make sure it's right?" This is where things got a little odd. I thought his last comment was off because his tellers would have counted it twice already, and I trusted in their ability to count a fairly small $10,000 withdrawal accurately. But whatever.

We walked to the side room and started counting out the money bill by bill. Let me tell you, if you've never held $10,000 in your hands at one time, don't let it be the first time when you're in front of your banker because, trust me, you will get a little giddy! Money is emotional. It shouldn't be. It's just paper. But when you're holding 10,000 bucks in your hands, and that's 3 times greater than your own personal net worth, let's be honest, you might start giggling a little. I tried to hold back the smiles. I felt a little bit like a fool, with my banker staring at me. But he knew what was going on inside my head. I think he just wanted to see my reaction. Maybe he was feeling me out on whether he had made a smart bet on me or not. Yes, be

RICK·I·PEDIA
The Business Encyclopedia

Net Worth

Add all your assets together like cash, home value, personal property value, etc. Then subtract out all your liabilities and debt. (Don't include non-contractual bills)

excited that you've opened a store, but also realize that your worst day in business, bankruptcy, is always around the corner. Staying in business should be what

Of all the restaurants that are opened, 50% of them fail in the first year. Of the remaining ones that survive, 50% of those fail in the second year.

makes you giddy, not taking out the first loan that you'll owe back to the bank a year later.

One of my buddies owned a small coffee house chain. I saw him one afternoon and he looked a little more lively and quick than normal, a little lighthearted. I asked him what was up in his life to bring about this visible change in his demeanor. He told me that he had just success-fully exited his business, selling his ownership to one of his store managers. It just felt nice having the burden of business off his shoulders, and out of his checkbook. I was floored! He had been so proud of his new-age all natural coffee houses, but on that day he seemed to be almost celebrating. That's when he taught me a life les-son I'll never forget. He said, "Rick, it's true that when

SENSEI SAYS

If drive your business you do not, driven out of business, you will be.
— B.C. Forbes

you start your business you have this 'High.' Your best day in busi-ness is your first. But, after that it gets tough. You're second best day in business is the day you sell." I looked at him, knowing that for him and his family the exit was the right move.

I've heard this lesson from other successful people a few times since, and look forward to testing it out myself in a few years. I'm not going to tell you that all entrepreneurial scenarios will follow my buddy's "first-day, last-day" model, but most will. When people get excited about launching their new venture, they often cannot see the day to day difficulties that they will face in the trenches of business. They get a little giddy. So, enjoy the moment, that first day in business. Ones like it won't come around too often in life. Then get to work and build something you can successfully exit from in the future, enjoying that second best day in business.

Proverb # 2

Don't focus on what you're going through; think about where you're going.

hen I first opened my store I had a chamber of commerce grand opening ceremony where smiling, supportive fellow business people came over and ate donuts (I definitely knew how to put together a spread!). When they walked into the store they saw my layout. My wife, brother, and I had worked for a few months on getting the store ready to launch, but we were still low on inventory. All three of us were attending the local university and had compiled our personal textbooks to launch the store. I had 24 shelf units, and a whopping 12 books. You could see it on my honored guests' faces: "this guy's going out of business. Let's get over to the next grand opening, FAST!" I tried to make them feel welcome and excited, but they kept asking me, "where's your inventory?" I told them, "well, my business plan says that next month as the current semester ends, I'm set up to buy books from students to sell in the upcoming semester. So, I don't have much inventory yet. Students will be my main source of inventory, and then I'll order supplementally off various book websites as the next semester approaches." I could see them rolling their eyes, literally. They didn't know where I was going with this. They couldn't catch my vision. They only saw what they saw, and at that point I had practically zero products.

Wayne Gretzky famously said, "A good hockey player plays where the puck is. A great hockey player

---

Rⁱᴄᴋ·ⁱ·ᴘᴇᴅⁱA
The Business Encyclopedia

Seasonality

The fluctuations in business that correspond to changes in the seasons.

plays where the puck is going to be." I've found that when you are building a business you have to tell your story to your accountant, your banker, your mentors...be-

Nintendo was first established in 1889 and they started out making special playing cards.

cause people don't always see where the puck is going. What made Gretzky great was that on the ice he could see the future. Successful entrepreneurs can always see the future a little bit. Obviously, I'm not telling you to go to a palm reader for advice, because entrepreneurship is not about fortune telling. It's about building a plan and following that plan. If you've done your research, thought through possible market swings, written out your business plan with thorough financial statements, and even awakened dreaming about how your ideas are going to solve the world's problems, then that plan becomes your own personal "Entrepreneur's Bible." Make changes as your customers' demands shift, but hopefully you'll be able to stay largely true to it.

SENSEI SAYS

A majority of men, failure they will meet. Lack of persistence they have. Fail to create new plans to take the place of old, they do.
– Napoleon Hill

On the other hand, if you burst into consciousness in a mad sweat from an entrepreneurial nightmare, then that may be a sign to reconsider. Some startups face major pivots in their business model before and after launch (see Proverb 63 for more info on "pivoting"). Sometimes the customers just don't walk in the door. Sometimes you have to shift within the industry or supply chain. But, don't talk yourself out of your entrepreneurial dreams. If the numbers in your financial projections were good going in, chances are you'll have good numbers coming out. Keep at it.

Proverb # 3

Everyone has at least one "Million Dollar Idea" every 10 years. What we do with them directly impacts our future.

 read a study years ago that explained how, on average, everyone has at least one "million dollar idea" every ten years throughout their adult life. That's five to seven BIG ideas per person, but unfortunately not everyone can take advantage of every million dollar idea they come up with. What stops us from reaching our wealth goals can be financial, emotional, or physical roadblocks. Sometimes it's family that takes priority, or maybe we're scared off by the risk inherent in entrepreneurship. Or, like a guy I once knew, we create a wild and crazy new product that can solve problems and help people, but then treat our great invention like it's a toy to be played with instead of as the heart of a real business system.

Listen to this fish story! We all know people who love to fish. My dad's one wish in retirement is to buy a bass boat and fish with the grandkids. Think about it. Quiet, smooth water on a private lake, as the sun sets on a warm summer night. Glorious!

One renown fisherman I met a decade ago, let's call him Joe, entrusted me with his secret method to catch the biggest fish in the neighborhood. In his younger years, Joe would go out at night in his bass boat with a black light he'd rigged to the deck. He'd shine that light down on the water, and you'd be surprised how many fish it would attract! My brother-in-law, an accomplished fish-

RICK·I·PEDIA
The Business Encyclopedia

Black Light

A lamp which emits long wave ultraviolet light and not much visible light.

erman, says fish are just plain dumb. Well, he ain't lyin'! Using his proven fish attracting technique, Joe would take home tons of fish each weekend, to the praise of his friends.

True OR **Farse?**

Over one million Pet Rocks were sold in 1975, making Gary Dahl, of Los Gatos, California, a millionaire. He got the idea while joking with friends about his pet that was easy to take care of, which was a rock.

His buddies tried for years to pry the details of his secret fishing spot or lure choice out of him, but he never told a soul about his fishing discovery.

Later in life, when he was working hard paying the bills at his 9-5, Joe went shopping at the local bass boat store and noticed something strange. All the new boats were coming out with black light add-ons. He couldn't believe it! Now everyone was going to be able to catch fish like he could! Hurt, Joe went home and told his wife the sad news. She sat there, thought about the situation, and then smacked him with the newspaper...hard! "You could have taken that stupid black light contraption to Bass Pro and made millions," she cried. Over all those years he hadn't recognized the entrepreneurial opportunity. He was having fun. He simply loved fishing at night. What's wrong with that?

SENSEI SAYS

Discipline it requires to turn interesting ideas and fledgling technologies into a company that continue for years.
– Steve Jobs

There is no right or wrong in this story. Fishing or making millions of dollars, they're both awesome! You can turn something you're passionate about into a money making empire, or you can just kick back and enjoy raking in the catfish. The question is, what will you do with your next 'Million Dollar Idea?'

Proverb # 4

Be ye doers of
the word, and
not hearers only,
deceiving your own
selves. - James 1:22

s I explained in an earlier proverb, when we were contemplating opening our first college bookstore, Linda and I were both going to school, taking 21+ credits, caring for our first son Ethan, working full time, and living in a flooded, cockroach infested basement apartment, where Linda's wedding dress got ruined. It wasn't fun. The St. Louis Cardinals were in the World Series that year, however, so I didn't really notice the cockroaches much, unless they crawled onto the TV. (Kidding, sort of...)

About that time, my brother was getting more and more interested in real estate. He wanted to buy foreclosures and rehab them, and then either sell them or rent them out, whatever made more sense. One exhausting day, he asked me if I would go see the Real Estate Officer (REO agent) at the US Bank nearest my school. I remember I was so tired that I was audibly winded while speaking to him. With heavy breath I responded, "OK...here's the plan. I'll dress up in a suit before school. After class I'll throw on my tie, run over to the bank and spend my short 20 minute lunch break talking to the REO agent instead of eating." I knew that after the meeting I'd have to go to work for the night, followed by heading home only to find Linda asleep. At least I'd have something to look forward to....doing

RICK·I·PEDIA
The Business Encyclopedia

REO Agent

Real Estate Officer, usually at a bank, that handles foreclosures or short sales. A contacts to have if you want to do well in the foreclosure real estate industry.

it all over again the next day (sarcasm intended).

I could hardly believe I was fitting this into my schedule! I followed up, still winded and breathless, by asking my brother if he would stop by a bank near his house and talk with their REO agent as well. He responded, "oh no, I have too much to do. I have to finish building out my basement, and then go work out at the gym. I haven't worked out in a week!" I was blown away. I went for broke, "what about tomorrow or the next day? Do you have any time this week to go talk to the banker?" "I don't think so," he replied.

I couldn't believe what I was hearing. He had brought his idea to me, and I jumped on board, even though I had literally zero time to work in this banker meeting. I would have had to skip eating in order to be there. I was already only seeing my wife 3 hours a week, and

SENSEI SAYS

Without continual growth and progress, such words as improvement, achievement, success, no meaning they will have.

– B. Franklin

he couldn't even take off from his workout schedule to pursue his own dream! I immediately realized he was a dreamer, and that's great. But if you're an entrepreneur, you have to be a "doer of the word, and not a hearer only, deceiving your own self."

I'm "faking stabbing" myself in the chest as I write this. It's heart wrenching looking back to see where I was at that time. Not everyone has to go through what Linda and I did to find his vision of success, but he's gotta dang do somethin'! Don't fall into "analysis paralysis" where you over analyze your business idea, sometimes for years, before taking the next step in writing your "Entrepreneur's Bible." And please, don't get lazy or distracted as life throws massive curve balls your way. Set your goals and stay on the path you've laid out toward success. If you keep going strong you're going to make it. Trust me on this.

Proverb # 5

People don't avoid starting businesses because it's difficult, they avoid it because it's difficult.

onfused yet? Launching a business takes time, money, creativity, and energy just to start. You may have an entrepreneurial vision, but implementing it is way tougher than dreaming it. Now, some businesses are easier to get going than others. For instance, building a steel mill versus opening a car wash, becoming a personal trainer, versus starting a home-based craft business. But no matter what your business is, you have to plan everything out, write your 'Entrepreneur's Bible,' prepare marketing materials, develop the website, get financing, build out your facility, etc.

Most people can get through the planning stages if they push themselves to make the time, do a little research, read a startup guide book, and talk to a mentor. It's the next stage in business that scares people away from entrepreneurship. See, people don't avoid starting businesses because creating an LLC or signing a short-term lease is difficult; they avoid it because they can feel the weight of all the hidden, tediously detailed effort on the back end that goes into actually running a new venture. The unknown, the day-to-day drama, and maybe the most difficult part: you have to trust that the 'Invisible Hand' will sweep through town over the coming years in your favor.

The 'Invisible Hand'...you gotta just trust it. I know, having faith in capitalism can be mentally and emotionally taxing. In the

RICK·I·PEDIA
The Business Encyclopedia

Invisible Hand

Individuals try to maximize their own good (and become wealthier), and by doing so, through trade and entrepreneurship, society as a whole is better off.

end, after all you've done, sometimes business success comes down to the market moving as it well, and the market can almost never be controlled. Do your best to weed out risks before

In 2011, approximately 400 deaths occurred in the United States due to workplace violence.

you go into business, and then fight to keep risks low throughout your entrepreneurial experience. If you've done your research and preparation, you are more likely to find yourself in the throes of success, but nothing is guaranteed.

Issues are going to pop up randomly throughout the startup process and every day after you open your doors. I'm not going to sugar coat it. Here's a window into the dark side of entrepreneurship:

1. Employee theft, no-call-no-show, and sex on the clock (this happens more than you'd think!)

2. Drug-deals and hobos in your parking lot.

3. The unfortunate result of having to liquidate and go out of business.

SENSEI SAYS

The chance to work hard at work worth doing, the best prize in life it is.

— Theodore Roosevelt

4. Endless printer death (see Proverb 24).

5. The never ending incoming cold call business-to-business sales mania. They will find you!

6. Crazy customers who scream and drop the f-bomb repeatedly.

7. Electrical blackouts, software crashes, and plumping backups...OH MY!

8. Operational responsibilities (opening, closing, hiring, firing, etc.)

9. Excess inventory, displaying inventory. Heck, inventory in general.

10. Having to create systems to solve problems, ALL THE TIME!

These daily struggles and many more are the reason so many people take the perceived safer road of employee rather than employer, never starting their own little something. Sure, writing your grand idea on paper is one thing. Living it is another. The ten issues listed above and many more will be thoroughly explained in my upcoming book: *The Dark Side of Entrepreneurship*. I hope the threat of these problems won't deter you from your entrepreneurial dreams. I'm just being honest. Nobody said entrepreneurship would be easy, they only promised it would be worth it.

Proverb # 6

When you think you've found your niche: test it, research it, and if it feels right, GO FOR IT!

 few years ago, my wife Linda and I were both working full time, going to school, taking 21+ credits per semester, and raising our son Ethan. We lived in a basement apartment with HUGE German cockroaches, regular flooding, and no kitchen. Ethan, was actually sleeping in the closet. Things were a little tough as we lived paycheck to paycheck. I only saw my wife for three hours a week during the brief moments we swapped Ethan back and forth between classes and work.

During this hectic time, I was constantly looking for opportunities to make money. My goals at that point were to move out of that basement, finish school, and get more financial stability for my family. So when I saw that the university didn't sell used books, but still used the new-only bookstore model from the 70's, I knew there was an opportunity to make money. To my surprise, the school did not buy back many textbooks either, leaving students to fend for themselves in liquidating their unwanted course materials.

If the truth be told, when I started my business, I didn't want to be a librarian. I didn't even really like books. However, our decision to open a bookstore wasn't about us; it was about noticing the under-served and

RICK·I·PEDIA
The Business Encyclopedia

Annualized Rate of Return

The return on an investment over a period other than one year (such as a month, or two years) multiplied or divided to give a comparable one-year return.

unsatisfied custom-
ers in the local colle-
giate textbook mar-
ket. Anytime there is
a demand larger than
the supply of a prod-
uct or service, peo-
ple will get creative

True or **Farse?**

Business stat: 80% of startup
businesses that launch with a
business plan are in business at
the end of that same year.

in trying to solve their own problems. These efforts
always breed huge inefficiencies, but it's better than
the alternative of going without. I was walking down
a hallway at school when I noticed cork boards filled
with "textbook for sale" postings. Some students would
cover other students' ads with their own; others would
rip off all the phone number tabs of their book-selling
competitors. (That's about as ugly as it gets for a small
town university in middle America...wink).

My wife and I did surveys across campus, measuring the
true demand for an off campus, used textbook store. We
started buying and selling books out of our basement,
using $300 I had borrowed from my brother, promis-
ing him a 120% annualized rate of return over the two

SENSEI SAYS

Owe the bank
$100, your
problem it is.
Owe the bank
$100 million, the
bank's problem
it becomes.
     - J. Paul Getty

months that we'd
need his money. It
sounded like tons
of money, but re-
ally, it was only
$60 bucks inter-
est. Two months
later, I did what I
said I was going
to do and paid off

our $360 loan. He was shocked! Since he had thought he would never get any of his money back, the $360 was a nice surprise (thanks for the faith in us, bro).

Our surveys checked out. The students definitely wanted a solution to the cork board fiasco. And our test run of buying and selling out of our basement that first semester was hugely successful. It was about this time that Linda and I knew that this was going to be a good deal for us. So we moved forward. I wrote my marketing plan as an honors project in my Principals of Marketing class and my financial plan as an honors project in my Corporate Finance class, killing two birds with one stone, and having a blast doing it! My professors and university administration were fully behind me, so my fears of failure were greatly reduced. If the faculty on campus were willing to spread the word, I knew my target customers would walk in the door. Everything just fell into place and the deal felt right, even to Linda, my cautious, business-savvy, spouse. The final step was getting the loan now, but that proved to be more difficult than I expected.

Proverb # 7

To be successful you often have to open up and bring people on board.

very time I teach a college entrepreneurship class where students have to develop a business idea, they tell me how they want to keep their ideas to themselves and not share them with their friends or other students. I respond by saying, "snowboards. There. I just thought of them. Now, don't take my business idea! I'm gonna make millions!" Just because you have a good idea doesn't mean you can physically, mentally, or financially develop it. A wise man said that if you truly want to understand something, you have to:

1. Meditate on it.

2. Write it down.

3. Tell someone about it.

Action is required to take any idea to the next level. If you come up with a great new technology or widget and don't do anything or tell anyone, you're almost certainly condemning it to death. It'll remain a dream. So start brainstorming about both your idea and implementation plan. As I explained in the introduction, write down your ideas in an Idea Notebook. I have one of these little black spiral Idea Notebooks in the console of my car at all times, so if I get a brilliant (and often fleeting) idea, I can scribble it down right away. I know several successful serial entrepreneurs who

RICK·I·PEDIA
The Business Encyclopedia

Inventory Controls

Operations put in place to supervise inventory, ensuring product levels are adequate to meet demand without excessive oversupply while guarding against shrinkage.

regularly fill up their own Idea Notebooks with all types of things—website and app ideas, to do lists, and the occasional strains of genius. Logo concepts are jotted down regularly.

True OR Farse?

A 1907 study concluded that the easiest color to spot is yellow. This is why John Hertz, the founder of the Yellow Cab Company, picked cabs to be yellow.

They're often hideous, but the whole process is part of keeping our minds sharp and alert, always looking for the next big deal.

Later I take these rough entrepreneurial visions, call my friends, mentors, and fellow entrepreneurs, and divulge every last bit of creative thought to them, asking for feedback and guidance in the development process of the embryonic endeavor. Business grows by sharing with, not by separating ourselves from others. Rarely, non-disclosure clauses are necessary, but 99% of the time they're not. (And 99% of the time I make up my own statistics, so take it for what it's worth)

Note: If you don't do the little things first, people won't take you seriously, and you may go right out of business. So as you build your idea through collaborative effort, write a thorough 'Entrepreneur's Bible' detailing your plans for marketing, outlining your day to day business operations,

SENSEI SAYS

Big pay and little responsibility found together they are not.
- Napoleon Hill

breaking down your financials, and explaining your exit strategy. Bankers won't believe you when you superficially say you're going to succeed in business. If you don't start out detailed, you'll quickly end up sloppy, and everyone knows it.

The same thing goes for your accounting. If you don't have a strong inventory controls and accounting system in place for your business in the beginning, you've created a sandy foundation to build on. Things will get lost. Going from Idea Notebook to Business Plan takes organization and thought. I was both driven and lucky. I put together my detailed plan, wrote it out, and then rewrote it again and again. And better yet, I could explain it clearly. I had market surveys, home trials, realistic financials, and a great accountant. What I lacked was inventory controls. I can't tell you exactly how much money I lost from theft, misplacing inventory, miscalculating orders, etc. But one thing's for sure, it wasn't an immaterial loss, and I'm lucky it wasn't more. When starting a new venture, you need as many things in your corner as you can get. The fewer mistakes you make starting up, the faster you'll get financially stable, allowing your fledgling business to stay alive another day.

Proverb # 8

"Duree Knuckles"

s I was teaching a college entrepreneurship class one night, the fundamental structure of entrepreneurship came to me. It all fit together in my mind as one simple four-step process. I realized that most people go through these steps on their path to finding entrepreneurial success. After I discovered this insightful process that night, I quickly wrote down the four steps, and the next day I ran them by a few members of my team. They immediately labeled the process the "Duree Knuckles." I've been referred to as "Knuckles Duree" ever since!

To understand the "Duree Knuckles," you need to take your hand and make a vertical fist. Turn the fist up toward you and look at it. Point at the little pinkie knuckle on the bottom. That's the foundation of your fist, your entrepreneurial story. It's the "Make Money" knuckle. If you're an entrepreneur and start your own business, the first thing you have to do is make money. No matter what goals you have in life or what noble reasons you have for starting your own venture, without money you're going to be out of business quick with those goals severely threatened. You can come back from bankruptcy, but it's tough. I recommend against it. To keep your organization's foundation strong and realize long-term success you must "Make Money."

> ### RICK·I·PEDIA
> The Business Encyclopedia
>
> **Duree Knuckles**
>
> 1. Make Money
> 2. Teach a Man to Fish
> 3. Make Your Wife Happy
> 4. Give Back

Second, you have to hire people to build your team and expand your business. My dad always said the most charitable thing you can do for someone is give him

True OR Farse?

On average, 6 newborns will be given to the wrong parents daily.

a job and teach him a trade. It's our responsibility as entrepreneurs to train, mentor, and open doors for our employees, so they are able to take over the business in the future, or go off and build their own. I look at this as the old Chinese sage did, "give a man a fish; you have fed him for a day. Teach a man to fish; and you have fed him for a lifetime." Oddly enough, by building your team and expanding the business, you continue to follow the first knuckle of making money! The second is to "Teach a Man to Fish."

Now that your foundation is set and your team is built, you're ready for number three. The third knuckle up the vertical fist is to "Make Your Wife Happy," because, let's

SENSEI SAYS

See how little you can give for a dollar, do not. Use skill and imagination to see how much you can give for a dollar, and succeed you will.
– Henry Ford

be honest, you can't do anything unless your wife is happy. Build your life together, have kids, build a sustainable standard of living, and you'll be free to open your heart and mind fully to the last, greatest knuckle. But to recap, the third knuckle is to "Make Your Wife Happy."

The fourth knuckle is the largest on your hand and the most impactful of all. This top knuckle on your vertical fist is to "Give Back." We all have a lifelong responsibility to give, help, and serve those around us. Entrepreneurship accentuates that responsibility. "Of those to whom much is given, much is required." And be generous! Just look at Warren Buffett. He made over $40 billion in his life, and then gave away $35 billion of it to help people. Now that's what I'm talkin' about! The fourth and top knuckle is to "Give Back."

Service is what life is about. It brings great joy to all, but if your family isn't taken care of, good luck finding the time and money to help out consistently at the local boys and girls club. Or, if you haven't been a good steward of your business and employees, get ready to watch your funds and resources dwindle, leaving less for you to give. Follow the principles of the "Duree Knuckles" in your life and you'll most definitely find entrepreneurial success.

FARCE = On average, 12 newborns will be given to the wrong parents daily.

Proverb # 9

Get serious, find an idea, write a business plan...and GET GOING!!!

here was a girl who sat next to me at a call center job I had during college. Now to tell you a little bit about myself: I'm as open to the world as this book is that you're reading right now. I'm blunt to a fault and no topics are off the table. Whether I am at school, work, or home, everyone knows I'm into religion, politics, and entrepreneurship. This friend was no different. She turned to me and said she wanted to start a business. Immediately, I slammed the headset down, swiveled my chair and started to engage her. My creative brain was turned on and I got excited (C'mon now, focus! Get your mind out of the gutter. This is exactly how it went down). Here was someone else who wanted to be an entrepreneur, too! I asked her what type of business interested her. She leaned in sneakily and asked, "do you know what I really want to do? I want to open a restaurant because my boyfriend's whole family keeps telling me I make great meat. All types of steak, hamburgers, brats, and...did I mention steak? Oh ya, I can make up some great meat!"

I didn't know where to go with that. It was leaning toward inappropriate workplace conversation. Make great meat indeed, but I just went with it. I started to torpedo questions at her about her dream business. "What other foods will you offer besides meat? What's

RICK•I•PEDIA
The Business Encyclopedia

Brick-and-Mortar

Refers to a business' physical retail space that is open to the public. Often used when discussing "Mom & Pop" shops.

the menu look like? Will you be in front of a Wal-Mart or another discount store? Will you open a franchise or go with your own meat recipes? Will you have a steakhouse or a general

restaurant that also serves meat? What pricing will you set? How will you market to get the customers in the door? How will you succeed when most new restaurants go out of business in their first year? What logo or branding do you have in mind? Will you be the chef because everyone knows you make the best meat? Or will you be the waiter, the manager, or the book keeper? What atmosphere will you go for? Will there be a fast food option? What kind of seating will you have? Will you have space for corporate / party events?"

I was in the zone! My mind was coming up with questions faster than my mouth could spit them out. Then I began to notice her eyes glazing over and turning downward. I could tell I had overwhelmed her, big time, so I trailed off mid-question and just sat there waiting for her to come to grips with what had just happened. She had no answers for any of my questions. Finally she looked at me, smiled, and asked, "do you know what I really want to do? I want to write a children's book. I read to my niece and nephew at night, and they fall right asleep every time." I couldn't believe what had just happened. She had switched her dream business idea on the fly. Maybe the last conversation had become tiresome with all those boring details I was throwing upon her. Maybe she didn't like thinking about actually furthering an idea, building it into a full business venture geared to making money, and solving problems. I was taken aback, but I didn't want to go back to the phones in the call center, so I went with it.

I started asking her, "what companies are you looking to for publishing? Who's going to do your editing and artwork? Have you have any experience drawing professionally in the past? What academic training do you have in English or writing? Where are you going to market your books? Will you be on Amazon because a lot of the brick-and-mortar bookstores are going out of business right now. What age range are you going for? A five-year-old and seven-year-old read at vastly different levels." Once more I began to notice her eyes glazing over and turning downward. I'd done it again. Trailing off mid-question a second time, I just sat there... waiting.

Then she surprised me again. She looked up at me, smiled, and said, "do you know what I really want to do?" I was floored, to say the least! I don't even re-member what her third dream en-tailed, except that it had something to do with owning a mechanic shop together with her boyfriend. I had

SENSEI SAYS

Live their dreams many do not. Because stop living their fears, they cannot.
    - Les Brown

just dived head first into her brainchild, thinking she was a serious person, and realized a little too late that her business goals were going to be forever reserved for her dreams. It's not wrong to be a dreamer. I respect all types of financial and entrepreneurial goals, whether they are employee, contractor, or business owner related. But if you're just a dreamer and not a practitioner, I personally can't talk to you about your business ideas. I get too involved in the money making and expansion aspects. I spend too much energy on the dream that isn't, by its own definition, ready to be realized. Entrepreneurship is too intense a topic for me.

Don't mess around coming up with silly excuses as to why you can't move forward with your business idea today. Get going! Start writing down bits and pieces of your plan, get a mentor, and go online to read sample business plans in your industry to help organize your thoughts.

Entrepreneurial
MANAGEMENT

Proverb # 10

Complete college or trade school to prove that you can finish something.

**A** lot of entrepreneurs just want to go out there and do it. And as much as I want to say go for it, I find myself being reserved because even in entrepreneurship there are still dues to pay, due diligence to perform. One of my entrepreneurial idols, Robert Kiyosaki, grew up being mentored by his "Rich Dad," his best friend's father. Even though he was ready to launch a business at a young age he still pursued his education with the Merchant Marines. He understood that you always need a fall-back plan in life. There's something to be said for our traditional bureaucratic education system. The skills we learn in school can come in handy later on.

That said, getting a formal education can sometimes just be that piece of paper that gets you in the door showing you completed something. It may be that your particular degree doesn't directly help you achieve your entrepreneurial goals. You may have received a philosophy, history, English, or special education degree, but then end up starting a real-estate office. In this case, the courses you took for your degree may not have a lot of relevance to your business. But the fact that you fought through four or five years of higher education gives you an endurance bonus, goal completion experience, and the ability to meet

RICK·I·PEDIA
The Business Encyclopedia

Mission Internship
Independent study course for college credit, usually outside the country, helping others in physical and spiritual ways.

a deadline. Some-times business is just that straight-for-ward. You have to get something done on time for a customer. Turning in papers in school teaches you how to do that.

True OR **Farse?**

Dave Thomas founded Wendy's, helped save KFC, and was a high school dropout.

Time management is just one skill you can gain at col-lege. Another is confidence. For instance, if you are to go into international business sometime in the future, but have never traveled internationally, you'll most likely be very nervous. However, if you backpacked through Europe in college, volunteered a semester with the Peace Corps, or gone on a foreign mission trip, you can say you've traveled abroad and will feel a little more confident when international challenges arise.

Once you're out of school, never stop learning. Pay for weekend seminars, read interesting books, have kids...

SENSEI SAYS

In business, paid in 2 coins, each of us is. Cash and experience, our rewards they are. Take first experience. Later cash will come.
– Tony Robins

that'll teach ya! Don't ever stop. Entrepreneurship is about change and progression, moving with your market and customers. Learn whatever is needed to satisfy them, apply what you've learned, and you're on your way to becoming rich. Just for fun, see how some of your personal daily habits balance with the average millionaire's. Check yourself against Tom Corley's list of "Things the Rich Do Everyday" and see where you match up:

1. 70% of wealthy eat fewer than 300 junk food calories per day. 97% of poor people eat more than 300 junk food calories per day.

2. 23% of wealthy gamble. 52% of poor people gamble.

3. 80% of wealthy are focused on accomplishing some single goal. Only 12% of the poor do this.

4. 76% of wealthy exercise aerobically 4 days a week. 23% of poor do this.

5. 63% of wealthy listen to audio books during commute to work vs. 5% for poor people.

6. 81% of wealthy maintain a to-do list vs. 19% for poor.

7. 63% of wealthy parents make their children read 2 or more non-fiction books a month vs. 3% for poor.

8. 70% of wealthy parents make their children volunteer 10 hours or more a month vs. 3% for poor.

9. 80% of wealthy make Happy Birthday calls vs. 11% of poor

True or Farse?

Leonardo da Vinci could write with one hand and draw with the other at the same time.

10. 67% of wealthy write down their goals vs. 17% for poor

11. 88% of wealthy read 30 minutes or more each day for education or career reasons vs 2% for poor.

12. 6% of wealthy say what's on their mind vs. 69% for poor.

13. 79% of wealthy network 5 hours or more each month vs. 16% for poor.

14. 67% of wealthy watch 1 hour or less of TV every day vs. 23% for poor

15. 6% of wealthy watch reality TV vs. 78% for poor.

16. 44% of wealthy wake up 3 hours before work starts vs.3% for poor.

17. 74% of wealthy teach good daily success habits to their children vs. 1% for poor.

18. 84% of wealthy believe good habits create opportunity luck vs. 4% for poor.

19. 76% of wealthy believe bad habits create detrimental luck vs. 9% for poor.

20. 86% of wealthy believe in lifelong educational self-improvement vs. 5% for poor.

21. 86% of wealthy love to read vs. 26% for poor.

*http://www.daveramsey.com/blog/20-things-the-rich-do-every-day

No matter who we are, everyday we're either moving forward or backward, moving toward our goals or away from them. Are you regularly improving yourself? Are you doing what it takes to get to the next level? Gauge yourself and the growth trajectory you're on toward reaching your financial goals, then accelerate.

Proverb # 11

Be alert to business needs, then solve them quickly, efficiently, and effectively.

 great entrepreneur has the ability to take a scenario where no control systems exist and quickly create and implement a system of their own design that will be efficient and effective going forward. In the book Blink, by Malcolm Gladwell, we learn that, after only a few seconds of interaction, people can instinctively feel whether or not something is right or wrong without long-term research on the particular subject.

"The psychologist Nalini Ambady once gave students three ten-second videotapes of a teacher—with the sound turned off—and found they had no difficulty at all coming up with a rating of the teacher's effectiveness. Then Ambady cut the clips back to five seconds, and the ratings were the same. They were remarkably consistent even with she showed the students just two seconds of videotape. Ambady then compared those snap judgments of teacher effectiveness with evaluations of those same professors made by their students after a full semester of classes, and she found that they were also essentially the same. A person watching a silent two-second video clip of a teacher he or she has never met will reach conclusions about how good that teacher is that are very similar to those of a student who has sat in the teacher's class for an entire semester. That's the power of our adaptive unconscious."

If you want to succeed as an entrepreneur, you need to be able to recognize potential busi-

RICK·I·PEDIA
The Business Encyclopedia

Go with your gut!

Trust your initial feelings when faced with problems.

ness opportunities or threats quickly and respond competently by instinct. Sometimes you just have to go with your gut! It sounds weird, I know, but here's an

True or Farse?

Microsoft made $16,005 in revenue in 1975, its first year of operations. 25 years later Microsoft was the most valuable brand name in the world.

example of how this worked for me. When I first started my bookstore, my brother and I realized how few operational controls we had in place. Customers were coming in the door (Awesome!), but we were having a tough time acquiring inventory quick enough to help get the customers what they were asking for. Delays don't look good for new businesses. It stinks of unprofessionalism. Unfortunately, we quickly found that our ordering department was only part of the problem.

We needed operational help fast! Not only were we lacking inventory ordering and management systems, we needed a consistent pricing formula, categorized human resources procedures, and a work file management system. The operations plan I had written when I was developing the business was embarrassingly weak. You always mess up on something when you're starting a business, and one of my weaknesses was in operational controls.

SENSEI SAYS

Problems, you must identify. Focus power and energy to solutions, you must.

- Tony Robins

We decided right away to build Excel sheets to organize our inventory, scheduling, pricing, HR, etc. We used our best judgment setting up the documents, guessing how things should be categorized and displayed. Surprisingly, we still use those same Excel sheets today with very few alterations from the original files.

If you can't instinctively recognize a business need, and then solve that need quickly, efficiently, and effectively, you're gonna have a harder time in business than you'd like. This particular skill set is not something that you can easily learn. It has to come from your gut. Trust yourself when you're in a hard place at the office. You're the entrepreneur. You can solve problems. It's what you do.

Proverb # 12

You are what you eat!

You know the old saying, "you are what you eat." The basic premise of this tenet is that you become what you surround yourself with. Consumers say, "you get what you pay for." Fathers the world over tell their kids, "be careful who you hang out with," which in "daddy-speak" means, my daughter can't date until she's 30. Religions say it a different way, "avoid the appearance of evil," meaning don't hang out in dark alleys with gang-bangers packin' heat. That's good advice no matter who you are.

Well, this Proverb is true in business as well. Certain industries attract certain types of workers and customers. Years ago I was part owner in a nightlife entertainment directory website. I worked with several nightclub owners, musicians, rappers, bar owners, and "want to be" models. SPOILER = I've never been mislead in business by anyone so often as I was with this group of so-called industry professionals. Yes, there are many great brew pubs and nightlife venues that are staples in the community, and we can all name them off the tops of our heads because they're run by great entrepreneurs who have a desire to build up their neighborhoods and give back to their clients.

At the same time, however, the nightlife industry has a lot of "Joes" opening bars in order to get drunk. (Sorry, to all of you readers named "Joe.") They're not building an entrepreneurial

RICK·I·PEDIA
The Business Encyclopedia

Moonshining

The illicit production of high-proof distilled spirits.

empire to benefit an under-served market, or providing a desperately needed service. They want a place for their friends to come and party. And that's enough for a lot of these guys.

True OR Farse?

In the 13th century, Europeans baptized children with beer.

It seems like we're seeing nightlife venue owners go in and out of business annually. Occasionally there's a story on the news of one of them getting cited for illegal drug use or prostitution, or openly selling alcohol to underage college freshman. Because of this reckless and deviant behavior, they never actually become professionals. Some can't meet a payroll, consistently breeding a transient workforce. Many make verbal agreements that they conveniently forget the following week. Still others end up running out of cash right off the bat because they didn't properly prepare their "Entrepreneur's Bible". Many of them are just "Joes" moonshining. But whatever. To each his own.

SENSEI SAYS

Profit in business, from repeat customers it comes, who bring their friends they do..

– W. Edwards Deming

If the truth be told, it's OK to be a "Joe," and even though moonshine can make you go blind, there are some great venues still around today with their roots in the roaring twenties and prohibition. But if you're in business, there's an automatic level of professionalism, respect, and responsibility granted to you because of your entrepreneurial status. No matter what industry you're in, if you find yourself uncomfortably dealing with "Joes" like I did, chose another industry that matches your professional expectations to go into. Life will be a whole lot easier. For me, the nightlife entertainment industry just didn't make the cut, and I was out of it as soon as I got into it. Remember you are what you eat, and even though I couldn't do business with the club owners I'll still go back for the hot wings (YEAHAA!).

Proverb # 13

Focus more on maximizing your strengths than growing your weaknesses.

 his Proverb may sound counter intuitive, because people always talk about building up their weaknesses. But from what I've found, your weaknesses are just that, weak. You can work all your life on perfecting those, but they're still not going to be as great as your strengths. I say hire someone or bring on a partner who has strengths where you have weaknesses. Then you can have fun focusing on what you're good at.

There's this thing called comparative advantage. It's when a nation or business supplies a product they're really good at and trade it to another country or business that produces a different product well. The first business could spend a lot of resources on building up this impotent sector or product line, but instead they just outsource the service and acquire it from someone else who is more skilled, or advantaged, at it. I follow this model because I only have so much time in my day and I want to have fun! Doing something I'm good at makes me happy. Doing something I enjoy is easy. Doing something I'm awful at is like getting kicked in the groin; you DON'T want to go there!

The Pareto Principle is known as the 80/20 law. Eighty percent of your revenue comes from 20% of your customers. If the truth be told, the 80/20 Pareto Principle is not an exact science. For some

RICK·I·PEDIA
The Business Encyclopedia

Comparative Advantage
The ability an entrepreneur has to produce a good or service at a lower cost than the competition.

companies 90-95% of their revenue comes from 5-10% of their clients. But either way, this principle can help you realize that you should focus your efforts dispro-

portionately on your few high-spending customers and "fire" the lowest-spending customers, who are often the most needy of all your patrons. I don't mean seriously firing your clients, but make sure you are giving adequate service to your big spenders. Your time is too valuable to spend too much of it on minimally profitable deals. Intensify your relationship with your major revenue generators and you'll see your total revenue jump.

I've labeled myself the "80/20 Guy," but with a different take on the fraction. I'll dive into a new project full bore and finish it 80% of the way, and then randomly walk away from the project distracted and bored. For instance, I'll create an idea for a new business, build it up, bring on people to work on it with me, recruit a professional team around it, develop the marketing strategy, and, when we're 80% of the way there, I hand over the

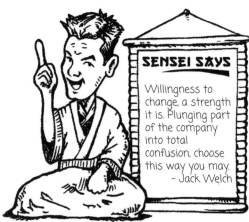

SENSEI SAYS

Willingness to change, a strength it is. Plunging part of the company into total confusion, choose this way you may.
- Jack Welch

reins to my people and run as fast as I can in the other direction, losing almost all interest in the project (DOH!). It's at this point I need someone to slap me. I know, it sounds like laziness. Well, guess what? It is. I'm baring my soul here.

What are your skills and what are your trials? For me, a big weakness of mine is not sticking with something until the ultimate end (Yes my wife already knows about this and she married me anyway). At the 80% complete mark I have to push myself consistently to stay on a project and finish it. Sometimes I walk away and hope that the system I have built can continue on to the finish line. Needless to say, I've dropped some balls in my day. I still have a car in my garage that is 80% street legal! Linda reminds me daily about it. But it's who I am, I'm the "80/20 Guy."

We've all got problems, we all have character flaws, yada yada yada. I don't take it too seriously. Life it too short to stress all the time about out flaws. But you have to know who you are. Don't lie to yourself. Bring people onto your team who can take over where you leave off.

Proverb # 14

Laissez-faire management isn't "lazy management."

ne day, out of the blue I received a letter stating that my store had won the local Employer of the Year Award. My team and I were ecstatic and set up a "business meeting" to go to the award banquet and receive this prestigious award. The place was full of local and regional entrepreneurs. These were some of the bigwigs of the community, and we felt honored to be listed among them. Other award winners included an owner of a fifty store chain of gas stations and a medium sized manufacturing company with several hundred employees. When we got up to receive the award, I commented that the reason, as far as I could tell, that our business was worthy of being labeled the employer of the year was because of the culture we had cultivated. At our office we implement a laissez-faire management style. Laissez-faire management isn't lazy management. It's liberating! If you're a laissez-faire manager, you believe that people will excel even when they are left alone to attend to their responsibilities in their own ways.

That night I told the other businesses in attendance that as the entrepreneur it was my responsibility to make sure that, if any of my employees wanted to learn jobs in other departments, they'd get that opportunity to grow and advance in the company. If any of my people want to know about the finances, I'll pull out the

RICK·I·PEDIA
The Business Encyclopedia

Self-motivation

Initiative to undertake or continue a task or activity without another's prodding or supervision.

official financial state-
ments and go through
our revenues and ex-
penses line by line,
teaching them the
income and balance
sheets. If they want
to use a new type of
social media to boost

True or Farse?

The number of Americans becoming
self-employed as entrepreneurs,
freelancers, contractors, or owners
of micro-businesses are decreasing
since the start of the Great
Recession.

our online presence, I'll get my marketing professionals
to sit down with them and listen to their ideas. If they
want to change pricing, the store atmosphere, bonus
structures, office procedures and operations, inventory
controls, wholesaling practices, online sales, business
technology, or whatever, I'm there to usher in their
creativity, as well as teach them all aspects of business.
Now, they don't always have great ideas for the store.
Spoiler: neither do I. But, we work together to serve
our customers and solve problems. There's no better
way to work than that.

Granted, all people are different. Not everyone excels
from a hands-off leadership approach, but it seems to
work at my stores. It allows my employees to perform
without intense supervision or regulation. If they're
dependable, honest, consistently busy, and accurate
, I don't look over their shoulders. I give them space
and expect maturity and self-motivation. I want them
to be creative, act "intrapreneurially" within their departments, and love what they do. Often, this kind of
leadership allows my teams to develop more efficient
operations and customer-centered policies. Plus, it's
a great way to keep employees longer. They feel like

they're really contributing to the success and growth of the company. Why do it all yourself? Build your team and give them some leash.

Alternatively, Micro-Management incorporates a more hands on oversight of each individual employee and/ or project. This management style is important when you are facing time crunches and need to push your team to meet deadlines. It also helps if your employees are less self-motivated or competent. Neither the Laissez-faire Management nor Micro-Management style is right or wrong. Each business will demand a different focus at different times. So listen to both your customers and employees, and do what works for you to build your company culture. Ask yourself, which management style do you think fits your personality more? Which will you implement more often? Which will make you more money in the end? Again, there's no right or wrong here, but it's important to know yourself, if you're going to lead people.

I heard a story once about Henry Ford's management approach toward one of his intrapreneurial employees.

SENSEI SAYS

To motivate other people, nothing more than management this is.
- Lee Iacocca

I can't remember his name, so let's just call him Joe. Joe was sharp! As you know, Henry Ford is known for the assembly line. Joe was a team lead in one of the manufacturing departments on the "Model T." Noticing some major inefficiencies in the system, Joe took the liberty of rearranging the department and employee responsibilities. His line's productivity went through the roof, and Mr. Ford knew he'd found a keeper. Noticing Joe's aptitude for creative problem solving, Ford transferred him to another department, with the mandate to reorganize the department however he saw fit. Can you guess what happened? Productivity in the new department skyrocketed as Joe engaged his "ambitious monkey" mind (see the introduction) developing efficiencies.

Henry Ford had well placed faith in his team throughout his career, giving a select few intrapreneurial leaders wells of authority to create and innovate in their respective departments. He successfully fostered a solution-focused culture at Ford Motor Company, one that bred efficiency, yes, but also high levels of employee satisfaction. Because of these entrepreneurial opportunities to remake departments as he envisioned, Joe knew he was making a real difference within his sphere of influence. How often do employees experience that level of contentment and satisfaction at work?

As entrepreneurs we have a higher calling than simply to direct labor and capital. Remember what the Big Guy upstairs said, "for unto whomsoever

RICK•I•PEDIA
The Business Encyclopedia

Intrapreneur

A person who while remaining within a larger organization uses entrepreneurial skills to develop a new product or line of business as a subsidiary of the organization.

much is given, of him shall be much required." We are creators, builders, developers, givers. It's our pleasure to teach and mold our employees to be entrepreneurs themselves, to give them all the tools necessary to start their own venture when they're ready, and even to be there as possible investors. Hire the right people, give them space to govern their own duties, help them learn all areas of your business, and see where they take you. You won't achieve your entrepreneurial dreams until you lose yourself in service to others. Trust me on that.

Proverb # 15

If someone comes to visit you, take them out to eat lunch.

I was at a county-wide Chamber of Commerce dinner recently, and was seated next to a lawyer I'd been referred to in the past. I didn't think I needed any legal aid, but not being the shy type, I started up a conversation with him anyway. We spoke about regional developments and city growth. I told him I had four businesses but didn't have a lawyer on retainer, to which he replied, "take me out to lunch one day and we'll talk about your businesses' legal needs. For the price of lunch, we'll chat."

I'm a go with the flow kind of guy, so I said, "sure, I'm buyin'!" I live by the law that if someone spends the time to visit you, show your appreciation by taking him out to eat. Again, I didn't have any legal needs to speak of, but since I couldn't let this upcoming lunch I'd be providing go to waste, I began planning fast what type of off-handed sexual comment I could make at work Monday to create some legal issues (only partially true). The conversation continued, and I tried to bridge our professional differences by stating that the local university was thinking about adding a new law school. He paused and frowned a bit. Had I offended him? I had thought that maybe by appealing to his industry we'd hit it off. But no. He got serious, turned to me and said, "what we really need is an engineering school." "Yes!" I exclaimed in total agreement. "We need more 'STEM' majors

RICK·I·PEDIA
The Business Encyclopedia

STEM

Science, Technology, Engineering, and Math

coming out of college," he continued, "people that can start technology businesses and create good paying jobs." I was blown away. Not only was this guy not an ambulance chaser, he had an entrepreneurial heart!

True OR Farse?

Thirty-five percent of the people who currently use personal ads for dating are already married.

The next minute, he was being introduced as the Chairman of the county's Economic Development Center. I found out that he knew all the movers and shakers in town, and was actively charitable in the community. With all the small business networking I was doing, knowing this guy was going to really boost me to the next level. I'm glad my knee-jerk reaction to pay for lunch came so easily, even if I didn't know at the time who this gentleman was I was going to be eating with.

It turned out that I didn't need to risk getting a workplace violation after all. There were tons of community building projects for us to start working on, and our entrepreneurial relationship is still growing. You never know who you're going to meet, so meet everybody. You never know whose services you're going to need, so keep a

SENSEI SAYS

Missed by most people, opportunity is. Dressed in overalls and looks like work, it does.
— B. Franklin

big Rolodex handy. Often in business, it's not what you know, but who you know. Random business relationships can turn into intriguing business projects worth real money. Don't short change yourself by sticking to your inner circle. If you have fewer than 300 Facebook friends you're not doing your job. Break open your shell, open your mouth, glad hand a few chaps, and build up your professional network with new friends. And don't be too cheap to pay for lunch.

Proverb # 16

Be humble. There's only one Albert Pujols after all.

Sorry if I crushed your ego with this Proverb. But when it comes to business you have to always be honest with yourself. If the truth be told, it probably won't be you personally that makes the business successful. The system you create will make the business a winner. For instance, no matter how hard you try, you won't be a better baseball player than Albert Pujols. He's the best. He's the one. He's "El Hombre." Be honest with yourself, and watch your pride level. Know yourself in and out. I don't want to hear you say you're gonna hit more home runs than Pujols simply because you're you, even though you're the best "you" you can be.

I'm not trying to be negative here. It's just that in business it's not about you, it's about the business system, the customers, your team. Example: Let's say you want to start a restaurant, and a location just opened up where a previous restaurant didn't make it. After doing your due diligence, you find that this was the third restaurant that has gone out of business here in recent years. Now, if you say that your restaurant will succeed in a building that has seen three restaurants fail over the last three years, you're playing against the odds, even if you are a great cook. It's pretty obvious that the restaurant gods hate that location.

RICK·I·PEDIA
The Business Encyclopedia
Albert Pujols

In his first ten years of baseball, he got...
- 3 MVP Awards
- 2 Gold Gloves
- 6 Silver Slugger Awards
- Rookie of the Year
- 9 All-Star appearances
- 3 World Series tours, winning 2 of them
- Only MLB Player to have more than 30 HR's, 175 Hits, .300 BA, and 100 RBI's in each of his first 10 years.

If you still choose to give it a go with that building, you may succeed, but it'll be tough, that's for sure. You'll have to develop some aggressive market penetration techniques and have

True OR **Farse?**

The only two days of the year in which there are no North American professional sports games (MLB, NBA, NHL, or NFL) are the day before and the day after the Major League All-Star Game.

a lot of cash on hand to endure possibly weak sales for the first year as you're getting going. But why take the tough road? Trust me, save yourself the trouble and don't go against the odds in business. It may pay off sometimes, but more often than not, your business venture is going to fail. Best case scenario, you will

SENSEI SAYS

A combination of war and sport, business is.

– Andre Maurols

lose money and go through mental turmoil, maybe for years. Take risks in business, but watch the odds. Don't say you will succeed just because it's you. Remember, there's only one Albert Pujols.

AND NUMBER 5 IS UP TO BAT...

IF HE GETS THREE STRIKES ON HIM, HE'S OUT!

NEVER GONNA HAPPEN.

FONY

Entrepreneurial
FINANCE

Proverb # 17

Be thrifty, but don't be cheap. Value quality over quantity.

hen I was a kid my family was poor. It wasn't just that we didn't get allowance, we didn't have access to cash whatsoever. My dad worked three jobs all through my childhood trying to make ends meet. All of us seven kids wore hand-me-downs and slept three to a room. My mom would grind her own wheat to make homemade bread. Now, homemade whole wheat bread is to die for, and I don't regret learning the value of a dollar when I was young. Just know that it was tough sometimes.

All of us kids looked forward to our birthdays each year, and not just because of the cake and ice cream. It was a well known fact that Grandma would open the wallet and bestow upon us the glorious $10 bill to spend as we liked. I remember watching Willy Wonka and the Chocolate Factory and seeing him open up that chocolate bar with the golden ticket. Birthday cards from Grandma were kind of like that. That was the most money I would see all year. My brothers would spend their birthday treasure trove on candy, Taco Bell burritos, and other consumables. Don't get me wrong, I love me some Taco Bell. I lived on it for years in college. But, for my one chance at cash for the year, I wanted something that would last for months. It represented the entirety of my financial livelihood. So, I went to the store and bought a He-Man Slime Pit for $10 and brought

RICK·I·PEDIA
The Business Encyclopedia

Allowance

Cash given to kids weekly to bribe them to do their chores, be nice to their sister, or just shut up.

it home. (He-Man rocks!) I felt like this purchase was a wise use of my severely limited funds, but my mom saw the tower and looked confused. "Why didn't you buy candy with

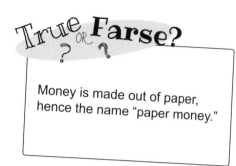

True OR Farse?

Money is made out of paper, hence the name "paper money."

your money?" I said that I didn't want my present to be gone in a few days. I wanted it to last months, so I got a Slime Pit, an obvious conclusion. I learned early in life the value of money, and decided while I was young to pool my cash for purchases that would last, rather than to spend my money on items offering immediate gratification like a piece of candy.

One night when I was 16, my buddy started tossing all his extra change out of his car. I asked him incredulously, "why are you throwing away that money!?!" He said, "it's only quarters, no biggie." The conversation with my mother from years before about the value of a dollar immediately flooded my memory. Knowing that

SENSEI SAYS

If lose yourself in something big, you can, more energy you will have.
— Norman Vincent Peale

there were no He-Man figures going for this little bit of change, I jokingly responded, "but you could buy 5 pieces of candy with a quarter!" He laughed and said a quarter was no money at all. I tell ya, I just see money differently.

However, just because I respect the buying power of money doesn't mean that price is the only motivator in my purchase decisions. Quality is also a major factor in determining what products I bring into my store. I try to buy high quality, long-lasting items for as low as I can find them. When you're faced with business needs, you can't always go with the cheapest product. Go with what is going to last, and have the right tool for the job. I've damaged pocket knifes trying to open boxes when I should've used a box cutter. Why didn't I have a box cutter? I was trying to save money by not buying one. That's silly. Also, sometimes we find ourselves standing in front of the office supplies aisle price shopping in order to save a few pennies. We could stand there for an hour comparing the various features of a stapler. I'm speaking from experience here. We need to spend our time more wisely. Buy the good one. Come on, it doesn't cost that much more. Be happy you have your time, your health, and a good product the next day. Or you'll find yourself running to the store the next day when you're slammed with customers to buy a new stapler.

FARCE = Money isn't made out of paper; it's made out of cotton.

Proverb # 18

Contrary to popular belief, successful entrepreneurs don't build large vaults filled with gold coins and swim through it like Scrooge McDuck.

et's get one thing straight. Entrepreneurs don't sit around counting their cash with evil grins on their faces. This dark picture of financially successful business people has got to change. Now, don't get me wrong. I'm the first one to say that the rich need to give back more. That's the top goal from "Duree Knuckles" (see Proverb 67), and there's no shortage of need out there. Opportunities to give are all around us. Great nonprofits are sprouting up across the country, churches are constantly looking for areas to serve, and communities are growing economic development resources to assist wherever possible. But culturally we need to stop being mad every time someone else makes it big. Acquiring wealth is not a competition.

I heard a story about a real estate tycoon, let's call him "Joe," who made good money during the real estate boom of the 2000's. He was being interviewed by a journalist one day and happily explained, "I made $1,000,000 last year and didn't even pay any taxes!" The interview was relatively normal, no odd questions or "gotcha" remarks, and Joe waited eagerly for it to be published the following month. When it finally hit the newspaper rack the headline

RICK·I·PEDIA
The Business Encyclopedia

Paper Profit (Loss)

Unrealized capital gain (or loss) in an investment calculated by comparing today's market price of a security to the original purchase price. NOTE: Gains or losses only become realized when the security is sold.

read, "Real Estate Tycoon Makes Millions, Pays No Taxes!"

Now, if you were having lunch with a millionaire and he said that he'd made $1,000,000 and didn't

True or Farse?

It takes about 63,000 trees to make the newsprint for the average Sunday edition of The New York Times.

pay any taxes on it, what would your next question be? I'd ask, "how the heck did you not pay taxes on those gains!?! Teach me oh wise one!" The journalist did her job of reporting the story, but didn't probe deep enough to find out the core of Joe's strategy that helped him make so much cash without facing tax penalties. The truth was, he hadn't made $1,000,000 in cash. His massive property empire had simply appreciated during the height of the real estate boom, and all those gains were paper profits only. No sale had been made, no money had been realized yet, so there was no tax liability.

Rich guys and gals don't build large vaults filled with gold coins and swim through 'em like Scrooge McDuck.

SENSEI SAYS

Distinguishes between a leader and a follower, innovation does.
– Steve Jobs

Don't have a negative knee-jerk reaction when someone tells you they've finally made it big with their business, or finalized a huge sale at work, or won the lottery. People are still people whether they have access to large sums of cash or not. We're all just "Joes" trying to make it. Support someone who gets ahead. If anything, ask for advice on how you can make $1,000,000 without paying taxes too! Successful entrepreneurs are often more than willing to give of their time to help someone else make it like they have. Build your advisory team with competent people. It never hurts to have a few millionaire supporters.

Proverb # 19

Get 'cho money!
(it's not as easy
as it sounds)

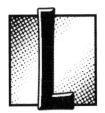 ending isn't always cut and dried. Every lender has their own risk levels approved by management ,but based on how much you need and what you're bringing to the table, they may choose a different lending tool than you expect. The graphic below shows some examples:

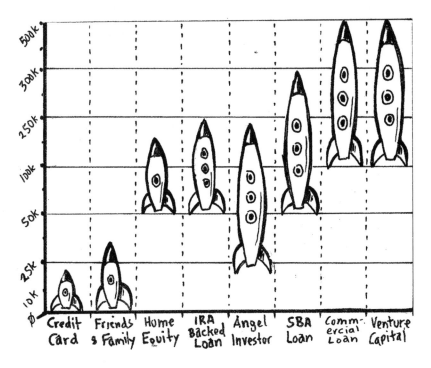

Knowing how much money you need will help the banker decide which avenue to pursue for your financing. If you need less than $50,000, bankers will often refuse the loan entirely, expecting you to get that amount from personal savings, family and friends, and credit cards. If you need between $50,000 and $500,000 for your startup or young company and have limited inventory, a partially secured government backed Small Business

Loan (SBA) is often selected. For the big money, startup loans over $500,000, you'll need a lot of capital to put down and inventory to collateralize the loan. Compa-

Ancient Rome had a rent-a-chariot business.

nies in need of these larger loans but don't have the collateral to back them up often find themselves pursuing venture capitalists or angel investors for financing. Sometimes banks may join together sharing the risk of these larger loans if they really want to do the deal, but those situations are very rare.

When I was looking for funding to launch my first textbook store, I had $2,000 from my wife's grandfather as her inheritance and $2,000 of collateral in our car. I wanted $50,000 to start my business, but believed that, if I was extremely frugal, I could get by with only $25,000. That would have been a risky financial choice, but I needed to launch this idea ASAP, and would've made it work no matter what. I had faith in my "Entrepreneur's Bible" that a college bookstore was just what my university needed, and had done surveys showing the market support for my product. Still, cutting capital injections by half starting out is always dangerous, especially since banks usually do the same to sales projections when evaluating the risk factor of investing in startups. If my sales truly ended being half of what I was projecting and my loan wasn't big enough to carry me through the first year, I'd be out of business. It was that simple.

The first bank I went to turned me down flat. The sum I was looking for was too low for them to bother with me. Plus, they had a stipulation that borrowers have two years work experience in their industry before the bank could lend money to their business. My work experience didn't meet their lending criteria. I told them, "I've never worked in a bookstore before, but how hard could it be?" Bad first impression. Not what they wanted to hear. Be prepared to deal with banks' internal bureaucratic minutia when borrowing from them. It's taxing red tape, but necessary for them to be conservative with their money. The entrepreneurs I know get frustrated with banks, and some of them flat out hate their rules. But that's the game you are playing when asking to borrow their money. It's part of the deal, so just accept it and cope with it.

The next bank I went to wasn't actually a bank. The guy was basically a knee-breaking underground loan shark. They wanted 100% collateral for their loaned funds, and charged premium interest for the service. That basically means they wanted to take no risk on the loan, get asset collateral in exchange for the cash loan, and have a high interest rate on the borrowed money to boot. It was a bad loan option all around, and definitely not a win-win solution for my startup. We passed on the loan shark quickly, but felt like our time for finding a loan was running out.

I'm telling you now, don't get frustrated and fear-

RICK·I·PEDIA
The Business Encyclopedia

Capital Injections

An infusion of cash into a company often in exchange for equity.

ful when this happens to you. There will be someone who will see the light and lend you the money you're asking for. You just need to find the right lender. Have your "Entrepreneur's Bible"

SENSEI SAYS

Unpredictable, the finical markets are. Different scenarios you must have. Predict what will happen, you cannot.
– George Soros

(business plan) prepared and easy to follow. Have your financials sound. Dress well, and speak professionally. But above all, just keep trying. Go from bank to bank looking for the type of loan that best fits your scenario. Hopefully your banker can help you get creative with the lending products they offer. The bankers that go out of their way to make things work for their customers are the ones that build lifelong relationships in the business community and get referred to other entrepreneurs. If you ask for referrals from your mentors, you may find one of these lenders quickly, and not have to go through the long emotional hunt of finding a compatible bank.

When it came to my hunt for the right bank, third time's a charm. I went in there and explaining how great my plan was, effectively threw down the gauntlet. Ok, not so 'Conan the Barbarian' as I would have liked. No one died after all, and I was wearing a suit instead of animal hide. The lender was thoughtful and asked probing questions. He seemed to be really interested. "Maybe he actually likes my idea," I thought. He was easy to talk to and engaged, and he understood where I was coming from. This guy was golden. He looked me in the eyes and asked, "Rick, how much money do you need?" I paused and thought a little bit about the question, sweating, hoping not to say the wrong number. Unfortunately I low balled the deal. "I can probably get by with $25,000." He grinned a little bit and asked, "but how much do you want?" I daringly replied, "we'd be sitting pretty with $50,000." "You got the money" he said.

A weight was lifted off my shoulders. I'd found a partner for my startup. It was a great day! Getting the loan to launch my business was easy when I found the right team member, my new banker. I had the money to open the doors of my first store. I'm not going to lie to you and tell you building my business was all gravy from there, but getting the money was a major obstacle I had overcome, and I was ready to rock!

Proverb # 20

Arbitrage = one of the greatest generators of entrepreneurial energy (and profit) in the world.

I heard a story one time about a young stock trader that blew me away. It opened up my entrepreneurial mind to see what actually goes on in businesses every day across the world. Let's call the hero of the story Joe. (see Proverb 15). Joe the stock trader was in his mid twenties just out of college with a degree in finance. He was known to have a keen eye for investments, and was ready to change his stars and make his mark on the world. He moved from his small hometown in the Midwest to the speedy streets of New York City to try his hand at the market. Not a gambler, he liked to look deep into companies to see what they were really offering customers long-term.

One day, he noticed an agricultural company that specialized in hay selling its stock with a buyer's bonus attached. It specified that if you bought their stock for the $25 asking price, the company would give you a free bushel of hay it had shipped into the New York harbor. Being from the Midwest. Joe had worked on a farm and knew the ins and outs of hay, and he definitely didn't want any in his apartment. But this deal wasn't about him, it was about making money. He saw an opportunity. So, he bought as much stock as he could afford with his limited starting funds, received his certificate for the free hay bales, and off he went on the subway down to the harbor

RICK·I·PEDIA
The Business Encyclopedia

Arbitrage

The simultaneous purchase and sale of an asset in order to profit from a difference in the price.

to collect his prize.

Once he'd traded his certificates in for the hay, he now owned both the stock and tons of dirty legumes. You may think of this as an odd predica-

**True or Farse?**

7-Eleven sells 2,000 pots of coffee an hour, every hour, every day.

ment, but not Joe. He immediately hauled all the bales he could manage back onto the subway to transport them to the other side of Manhattan where companies were buying hay at $25 per bale to use on farms up-state. He dumped that hay as fast as he could, zoomed back to the stock exchange, and did it all over again.

Joe was at this for days before anyone else got wind of the arbitrage deal and started buying up the stock for the same purpose. The stock price soared quickly making this deal unattractive for his purposes, so Joe stopped his run. But he'd made his money while he could and was out nothing but the energy he'd experienced carrying all that hay around town, a friendly re-minder of his after school work back home.

SENSEI SAYS

In life, only a few things right you must do, if not too many things wrong you do.
- Warren Buffet

Places and people aren't that differ-ent after all. Cap-italism can work anywhere, wheth-er it's New York, a one-of-a-kind city that never sleeps, or on a farm in fly-over country. USA. Joe simply connected the dots between hay bale buyers and sellers. If you can consistently do this over time with hay or any other product/service, your wealth can become truly unimaginable.

Proverb # 21

Make your money while the sun is shining, 'cause it's gonna rain on all of us someday.

oom and bust economies, financial cycles, bubbles...no matter what you call them, there have always been ups and downs to economies since the world began. Tulip Mania, the South Sea Bubble, the Bull Market of the Roaring Twenties, the DotCom Bubble, and just recently the Housing Boom are all examples of violent instability in the market. So, how do you take advantage of what you cannot control? You go along for the ride. What else can you do? We are not going to redirect the market or stop it's wild movements. No matter what industry you're in, you're gonna get rained on someday, meaning that business ending calamity may strike at any time. Even if you fight through and overcome all the wrenches that are thrown into your business, in the end, the time frame to make money in your market will eventually pass. While the sun is out, and the market is looking bullish, and people are wanting to spend money with you, take advantage of the opportunity and make your money. Sell, sell, sell!

The opposite is also true. The old wise man Anonymous once said, "sell when the sun is shining and buy when there's blood in the streets!" That's what I try to go by. It's not pretty, but making money doesn't stop with the easy buy in a bull market. The best entrepreneurs also find ways to make money when the market is bearish after a crash, then

---

RICK·I·PEDIA
The Business Encyclopedia

Financial Bubble

An economic cycle where prices rise above their true value and will continue to do so until prices go into free fall and the bubble bursts.

riding the bull wave back up. It's not easy, and many people lose no matter which way the market heads. But, if you want to beat the market, here are three points to

True or Farse?

The total mileage driven by all U-Haul trucks in a year is enough to move a person from the Earth to the moon nearly 2,000 times.

help you weather the volatile economic storms ahead:

1. Have Excess Liquid Assets at Your Disposal

2. Know When to Buy and Sell

3. Don't Get Greedy

The real estate market during the Housing Boom was at its height before the bubble burst in 2008. Tons of real estate professionals and lenders made big money during the boom, but they weren't prepared for the collapse, and many lost everything. No one wins on all their investments, but if you can hang on to a reserve of cash, holding out till the worst of the crash is over, you'll often come out on top. Old Anonymous comes through for us again with another pointed adage, "Cash is King."

SENSEI SAYS

An expert, an economist is, who tomorrow will know why the things he predicted yesterday, happened did not.
– Laurence J. Peter

He wasn't joking. Any time financial crises hit, those who are prepared with excess liquid assets do well.

Look at the story of Joseph of Egypt. Seven years of plenty to precede seven years of famine. When the world was starving, Egypt had liquid assets in the form of food to trade with. Today we have Euros, Yen, Pounds, Yuan, and good old American Greenbacks to do our dealing with. Have a stash of cash under the proverbial mattress for a rainy day. If it was good enough for Joseph, it's good enough for you.

The great Anonymous also gave us this adage, "time is the great equalizer." Generally, it's best to buy when everyone else is selling because the supply is greater at that time, driving down prices. On the other hand, you should try to sell when everyone else is buying because the demand is hot, causing prices to be in your favor. It comes down to supply and demand...who knew! (kidding.)

Whether it's a bull or bear market, entrepreneurs have to have guts. No guts, no glory! My dad was my inspiration to become an entrepreneur. He always said he had a cast iron rear end, but I didn't know how important that was until I opened my first store. He'd get kicked in it or fall on it, but either way it was iron, so no big deal! Remember, it's gonna rain on all of us sometime. It's how you deal with the coming storm that defines you as an entrepreneur.

TRUE

Proverb # 22

If achieving only 50% of your projected sales will send you into bankruptcy, rethink your 'Entrepreneur's Bible.'

mall Business Administration (SBA) loans are great sources of capital when you are starting a new venture. Since the bank is more secured with the SBA guarantee attached to these types of loans, you're more likely to get approved. I used SBA loans for the first seven years of my entrepreneurial experience. They don't come without challenges, however.

When I was applying for a loan for my second store I had to submit seven years of projections along with the business plan. Now, almost nobody follows projections past even three years, let alone seven. But the government gets what the government wants, so I just made some estimates based off of possible increases in market penetration over time and submitted the financials. Preparing a strong 'Entrepreneur's Bible' for my new venture was vital, but by this point, getting the money was more important to me than the accuracy of my seventh year of financial projections.

Bankers also need projections. Not seven years worth, but honest extensive financials are mandatory to success in business. Recommendation: be conscientious and don't get cocky! Have two sets of financials. The first one is your blow it out of the water, best case scenario, aggressive financials. These are the ones you pull out first, smiling all the way to the bank, so to speak. These reflect your hopes of unbridled success. They're naive and most

R<small>ICK</small>·I·PEDI<small>A</small>
The Business Encyclopedia

Margins

Take sales revenue minus the cost of goods sold, then divide that by sales revenue.

likely unachievable in application, but on paper they ROCK!

The second set of financials are conservatively grounded, what you pretty much guess will hap-

True or Farse?

5% of the Russian government's income comes from the sale of vodka.

pen if sales aren't as bright and shiny as you want them to be. The banker will take the first set of financials, smile back at you, and immediately put them to the side. Hey, you tried. They'll then take the second set of financials, cut your sales projections in half, and if you can still make money with that dissection, you're almost guaranteed to get the loan. This is tough for a lot of new businesses that hope to live on the margins of profitability, since their numbers aren't that strong to begin with: restaurants, golf courses, taxi services, salons—good businesses that aren't generally able to institute huge markups on their products/services.

When you choose an industry to go into, try to choose one with larger margins. It's not always possible, but you're more likely to succeed if you have a cushion. And

SENSEI SAYS

Strength and intelligence, guarantee survival they do not. Responsive to change one must be.
- Charles Darwin

believe me, we all make mistakes, and miss projections, and hit stumbling blocks along the way. There are no exceptions. The real doozies I call "Professional Failures." So be conservative, understand where the bankers are coming from when they cut your numbers in half. Don't you dare take it personally! It's just business. Instead, use your energy to prove them wrong by hitting your aggressive numbers! Blow them away at your year-end evaluations.

That's what I did with my second store. I got the SBA loan squared away and launched the business. It was exciting! My brother and I took all the knowledge we'd gained from our previous five years in the business and opened a new location, without having to go through the growing pains all over again. Our first full year, however, ended in a $60,000 loss. I wasn't happy with that, but I was content enough, and cautiously optimistic for year two. My accountant, however, was not. "Rick," he bellowed, "what's going on with this new store!?! Talk to me. Tell me I'm missing something. Tell me I'm not seeing what I'm seeing with these numbers." He was a great CPA, but was worried that I had veered from my original fiscal plans and business model. I calmed his fears about the financials and reminded him again of my growth projections. Sure enough, our second year-end evaluations surprised him with nearly $85,000 net profit. "Rick," he bellowed once again, "this second store was a great idea!" (see Proverb 21).

FARCE = A full 10% of the Russian government's income comes from the sale of vodka.

Proverb # 23

Entrepreneur's are storytellers. Ninety percent of what we say is how we say it.

hen I was on the hunt for my first million-dollar loan, I went to two different banks in search of a strategic partner to grow my business. I had relationships with both of them, and appreciated how they worked with me through the loan process. They each knew my story, but still asked for a lot of detail about changes in the industry and my particular business model.

I explained my cash flow to the banker step by step. It helped both of us understand the tilts and sways of my business. I was fairly detailed. "We're going to buy THIS to help us make money THIS way. THIS is how we're going to pay you back." Don't be shy here! When you're talking to your banker you need to be a storyteller. You need to build a virtual image in his mind to help him internalize where you've come from, where you're at, and where you're going. Once you've sold him on your plans, he'll take your story, this vision you give him of your business, and try to sell his management on your loan. Sometimes a bank will accept or deny loan applications based on internal lending practices, but many times it comes down to your presentation. Remember, it's 10% what you say and 90% how you say it. The commercial bankers need to be able to sell you and

RICK•I•PEDIA
The Business Encyclopedia

Strategic Partner

Party with which an agreement is reached for sharing of physical and/or intellectual resources in achievement of defined common objective.

your business to their higher ups if you want to get any money. It reminds me of the theater: you have to play a part and they have to come along with you in the story. Some people think business is all about numbers, but I tell you it's not. Often, it's the vision you create that gets the loan done.

The bank that gave me this first million-dollar-loan strongly emphasized their desire to be relationship bankers. To go along with the main line of credit, they wanted to:

- Refinance my home loans

- Open car loans

- Do my credit card processing

- Open a corporate credit card for my store

- Open several manager-level credit cards

- Refinance my commercial property loans

They had caught the vision of my vibrant ever-changing company and came aboard ready to sail. If you can sell your story to an engaged, energetic banker then he can bring the heavy artillery in support as you fight through the trenches in business. I give a lot of praise to great bankers. Not so much to average ones. Great

True or Farse?

The story of Rudolph the Red-Nosed Reindeer was written in 1939 as a way to promote the Macy's Thanksgiving Day Parade.

bankers are invaluable in keeping your company liquid. Plus, they introduce you to countless Big-Wigs in hopes of growing your company and doing more business with you in the fu-

SENSEI SAYS

Define reality, the first responsibility of a leader it is. Saying thank you, the last. In between, a servant the leader is.

- Max de Pree

ture. Great bankers have your company's well being at heart and earn their pay ten-fold. They also happen to be regular suppliers of baseball game tickets. Gotta love 'em!

Proverb # 24

Be a good buyer

of things.

 major attribute I value in entrepreneurs is their ability to find the good deals. You'll be surprised by how often crap happens when you're simply trying to make a living. One second you're checking someone out, ringing that cash register, bringing in the dough. The next second you're POS system crashes and receipt printer spits out error messages for six or seven minutes straight. It's a whirlwind of insanity. Or, when you need a printer during the busiest part of your day, yours breaks down, and surprise, surprise, the back-up printer is crashing with software glitches. It's at these moments you wonder why you get up in the morning. You think to yourself "Don't I have employees for this?" The answer is NO. Fixing problems is your job. You'll find yourself having to go and get what you can get, probably paying retail price at the local office supply store. This has happened to me at least once a year since I opened my business. Maybe I have a Bad-Luck Genie following me around, destroying my electronics for kicks.

If you're not under that kind of immediate danger, a resourceful entrepreneur will regularly be able to find high quality, low cost deals. Remember, there are two ways to raise your bottom line, increase your sales or cut your expenses. An easy way to cut expenses is to find great deals when you buy. In real estate, for instance, you don't buy property hoping to make a profit by capturing appreciation in the future. You buy low at a price that allows you to realize profit today, where in the worst case scenario you'll still make money. With real estate the worst case scenario is either the

RICK·I·PEDIA
The Business Encyclopedia

Bad-Luck Genie

Similar to a Poltergeist, it is a manifestation of an invisible but noisy, disruptive or destructive entity.

market flat lining or even depreciating your property value. Remember 2008 and 2009 anyone? If you're buying smart, you'll buy low and sell high (see Proverb 21). I know it's the

The deadliest jobs in the United States are that of steel workers, followed by electrical line repairmen and roofers.

oldest advice in the book, but it's been around forever because it's true. Wise entrepreneurs seem to always say: "you make your money when you buy."

Speaking of real estate, my business had made my wife, Linda, and me some extra cash to invest right as the Great Recession was starting. We could've gone with the hedge fund managers and bought US Treasury Bonds, but where's the fun in that. Instead, we looked for new startups that needed help relocating and getting office space on the cheap. Now, don't get me wrong. We didn't start putting "Entrepreneurs Wanted" ads on Craigslist. That's for dang sure. You never know who you're gonna get with that approach. We simply kept our eyes open and ears to the ground, searching for the right deal to present itself.

After about a year, two different businesses run by two very different entrepreneurs landed on our radar. They both needed to move their businesses into our county to take advantage of the active urban sprawl that we were benefiting from, both needed cheap office space, and both needed a place to live. We had the cash available to help with these endeavors, so we decided to buy two properties and they'd rent from us. We came up with a four-point plan:

1. Find a home that meets the living standards of the renters while satisfying their business needs when utilized as an office.

2. Make sure the price is a good financial investment (with the market and interest rates down, that was fairly easy).

3. Agree to a rent-to-own deal where the renters will buy the property in the future when they could afford it.

4. Upon future sale, we would gain whatever appreciation was realized plus a minimal monthly passive income.

With the tireless help of our miraculous real estate agent, we found properties and placed them under contract at very attractive prices, prices that allowed Linda and me to keep the rent low so that these two entrepreneurs could afford to grow their businesses. Before you knew it the deals were closed and the renters moved in, immediately revamping the facilities to suit their housing and business needs. Sales were made and growth happened almost overnight. It was a wonder to see. I say again, we could have bought US Treasury Bonds, but these real estate plays allowed Linda and me to keep the rent low so that these two entrepreneurs could afford to grow their businesses. It truly was a wonder to see.

FARCE = The deadliest jobs in the US are that of loggers, followed by fisherman and then aircraft pilots.

Proverb # 25

Taxes Suck! What more can I say.

xpenses are heavy. They can weigh down potential growth, limit hiring, cripple research and development, stagnate an entire organization...and we all have them. Just because everyone hates them, let's look at taxes for a second. If businesses have to pay more in taxes, they'll have less money to do any of the following: hire more employees, slash prices, give raises or benefits to their employees, make charitable contributions to organizations and the community, develop their business operations, or expand their product lines. Choose a small business you can relate to and pose these questions honestly. From my own business experience, the lower tax rates of the 2000's allowed BOOK-X-CHANGE to keep about $15,000 per year that we would have paid to the IRS had income tax rates not come down.

Now, let's take that annual $15,000 and think about what can be done with it? There's no right or wrong answer here. All things being equal at my bookstore, I could buy a new point-of-sale software to set up a textbook rental program the students are asking for. I could lower prices across the board. I could invest the $15,000 in a new store expansion servicing a different university, providing jobs and a cheaper textbook option to students there. I could donate the mon-

RICK·I·PEDIA
The Business Encyclopedia

Point-of-Sale

The point at which a customer makes a payment to a merchant in exchange for goods or services.

ey to a great social need in the community. I could expand my product lines to include sweatshirts and other merchandise, the sales of which would require me to hire more people. As economic growth from any of these options began to explode, the tax revenues up the supply chain from the manufacturer to me and all the wholesalers and shipping companies in between would increase.

So you can be prepared, I've made a short list of some of the more common expenses a new business will face. This list is in no way exhaustive, but I want you to start thinking of what

True OR **Farse?**

The IRS employee tax manual has instructions for collecting taxes after a nuclear war.

you may face in your entrepreneurial journey so you can plan successfully: I could pursue any number of growth options...or I could pay that $15,000 in higher taxes. If the truth be told, at my store I actually chose all of the above growth options. Each year that I saved $15,000 in taxes I did one of the following: started renting textbooks giving the students the buying options they wanted, slashed prices, hired more people, opened new locations, gave more to charity, or expanded my product lines. In doing so, I actually made more sales and paid a lot more in taxes than I would have otherwise. We experienced an average 30% growth every year since we opened. Facts are facts, I had more funds available to grow my business as the government took less in taxes.

SENSEI SAYS

Make you rick, your salary does not. Your spending habits, save cash they can.

- Charles A. Jaffe

Political Question: Let's take the position that government, your life-long partner, spends money on important things that the citizenry needs, and must take that money from those who have it to do so. From that position, what percentage of the $15,000 I wrote about earlier do you estimate would actually go to provide the great benefits we receive from said government? Keep in mind that the government isn't known for efficiency or effective spending. Let's say that after going through the bureaucratic system, 65% of that money is actually spent filling citizenry needs. What would you rather have, $15,000 more each year to be managed by you, the creative thoughtful entrepreneur building communities, or a net $10,000 dispersed to public needs? You decide. And remember, there's no right or wrong answer here...(wink)

Entrepreneurial
MARKETING

Proverb # 26

Creating a NEW demand is much harder than simply supplying an existing one.

n the late 2000's, the option of renting textbooks became increasingly popular to college students. With all the expenses and compliances a company had to go through to get a system setup to rent books, I thought renting was cost prohibitive for the average off-campus bookstore. I was working at my college textbook store BOOK-X-CHANGE, when one day the market changed. It was like the wind, the students all of a sudden changed direction from wanting to buy used books all day long to asking emphatically for rentals. There were so many people over the course of a month inquiring about renting textbooks that I had to come up with an official response for my employees to tell them. I had been caught off guard unable to satisfy my customers, but not for long.

The people were telling me they wanted to rent. I didn't create the demand for cheaper rental textbooks, the students did. It was my job as the entrepreneur to answer their requests with an effective solution. To satisfy their needs, I focused like a laser on building the best rental system I could come up with. I spoke with wholesalers about their rental modules, and visited other bookstores to get ideas of how to implement and run a fully rental system. I bought a new point of sale system, updated all my computers, and greatly expanded my website services. I hired more employees, changed my marketing materials, revamped my

RICK·I·PEDIA
The Business Encyclopedia

"The Sticks"
Rural, country living, beyond the outer exurbs of a city.

pricing strategy, and vastly grew my inventory.

I spent nearly $1,000,000 in a single month to make my store into a full rental textbook outlet. Most

Humans are the only species that have sex for pleasure.

off-campus bookstores don't have the resources, insight, or gonads necessary to grow that much that fast. Have you ever spent a million bucks in a month on credit cards? It was "Brewster's Millions" ('80's comedy) at my office that summer, except we were buying mountains of books, not icebergs. My team did what was necessary to satisfy the demand the market had swung face first in our direction. We were responsive, and because of that we flourished in the changing textbook industry, opening three new stores over the following three years.

Speaking of being sensitive to customer demands, let's talk a little about putting yourself last and the customer first. It's a mentality you have to have. You can only pay yourself if you first make the sale. With the food service industry for instance, you wouldn't want to open a trendy expensive Mid-

SENSEI SAYS

Create demand, the hardest thing to in business it is.
  - Jim Elder

dle Eastern restaurant in "the sticks" of rural Missouri where I grew up, crossing your fingers and hoping that people would come eat your Gyros. "But once they try the food," you tell your spouse, "they'll like it and come back!" Chances are, unfortunately, you'd be wrong, and soon you'd be broke and sleeping on the couch. You simply cannot guarantee that customers will consistently wander in and buy your products just because, "you cook good meat." People I grew up with from "the sticks" don't even know what a Gyro is. You can't foresee that they'll love the food, and you certainly can't predict that they'll come back.

FREE ADVICE: If you want to go into the food business in my home town, instead of trying to create a new food demand because you love it, maybe just open a Waffle House. You'll smell like pancake batter and bacon, but you'll stay in business for the long haul. My people love us some Waffle House!

Proverb # 27

Be like Santa from the Miracle on 34th Street. If you can't serve the customer, send them to someone who can.

e've all seen this movie, the cute ol' Santa, the bratty little girl, the family story; this proverb is about serving people, not about chasing the almighty dollar. Treat people as you would like to be treated and you'll win customers' trust. Help your customers get served. No, this is not a basketball analogy. People really do appreciate the fact that you care if they are overpaying. If you happen to be a little more expensive, often times the customers will pay the little extra money for your products, if they feel you're being honest with them, and are considerate of their needs.

One random day in my bookstore's life a guy came to me and said he would soon be graduating from college. He was excited to share that he had shopped at my store all his previous four years of school. "Sorry to see you go," I joked, as I thanked him for his patronage. He asked, "do you want to know why I've been coming back here for four years straight?" I always look to survey my customers, in hopes of finding better ways to serve them. Intrigued by his question, I asked, "sure, where did we go so right as to win you over?" He said that the reason he had been so loyal was that as a freshman four years earlier, he had sold all his valuable books to the official bookstore on campus, and when they wouldn't buy his last few titles, he brought them

RICK·I·PEDIA
The Business Encyclopedia

Patronage

The financial support customers benevolently bestow upon a business for earning and keeping their loyalty over time.

over to my store to see what I would give him. These were old titles and he knew they weren't worth anything: the official bookstore had already told him as

True or Farse?

The famous jewelry store Tiffany & Co. was established on September 18, 1837 in New York City. The amount of sales that were made the first day were $4.98.

much. But he was giving me a chance to see if I could help him out with a few books.

As he explained the story to me, I actually remembered him from four years previous coming in the store. My policy has always been to give the students what they want, and when they come in with an armful of books, they want to leave with cash and an empty backpack. So I gave him $5 a piece for his old edition textbooks. It was 5 bucks. Who cares about 5 bucks in business? What you should care about is having happy customers walking out the door, remembering how they felt when they did that deal with you. Did they feel taken advantage of like many bookstores do with college students. Or do your customers feel taken care of? Even though at $5 I was losing money on some of those old editions, I knew I'd won over a customer.

SENSEI SAYS

Satisfy customers, and make money you will. Fundamental to you aim, this is.
- John Egan

He became what I call a "Converted Customer." He never went anywhere else ever again for books because he knew each time he stepped in my store I'd take care of him. I had earned his trust with a simple kind act. I had taken personally his need to sell his books and helped him out a little. And his purchases from me over the following four years obviously surpassed that $5 loss in the beginning of our business relationship.

Whether your entrepreneurial venture is with books, or at a mechanic shop, or in a recording studio, serving people is profitable, and not only financially;, it's good for your heart. I will always pursue ventures that make money. Remember that's the first knuckle of the "Duree Knuckles Life Lessons." But my motivation will never be solely cash based.

Proverb # 28

Believe in marketing...
it works.

hen I first took the risk and opened my store, I had no money for flashy signage or exterior remodeling to increase the building's curb appeal. I got a 4x8 banner to use as a placeholder for a store sign until I would be able to get the $8,000+ for an LED-lit channel letter sign. The banner was cheap, easy. I was worried about getting enough inventory for sales starting out; branding had to wait, or so I thought. I went for the flimsy banner look to save my cash (not recommended!).

After a full five years I finally got off my butt and made the hard decision to upgrade. I know, why did it take that long!?! Laziness. Distractions. All of the above. Remember, I'm the 80/20 guy (see Proverb 13). It's not an excuse, it just is. I sucked at marketing for years. There, I said it. It's still hard for me, by the way. Eventually I pulled the trigger and bought a huge double lit channel letter LED sign you could see from a mile away. Maybe I was compensating for the five lost years of signage.

RICK·I·PEDIA
The Business Encyclopedia

Advertising vs. Marketing

Advertising: The paid, public, non-personal presentation or promotion by a firm of its products to its existing and potential customers.

Marketing: The systematic planning, implementation and control of a mix of business activities intended to bring together buyers and sellers for the mutually advantageous exchange or transfer of products.

Anyway, I was at a business luncheon the following week and sat next to an attorney, who I found out had worked down the street from me for the previous half-decade. Never

True or Farse?

In 1894 the first big Coke sign was found on the side of a building located in Cartersville, Georgia, and still exists today.

met him before, but the conversation was going fine. I started to talk about my business a little, where I was located, the normal ice breakers. All of a sudden his face brightens and he exclaims, "oh, you're that new store that just went in!" Confused I said, "no, we've been there for five years." He said, "no, no! The new one with the big lighted sign!" Sheepishly I replied, "actually, I just put that in last week. My store has been there for five years, but I never bothered to get a real sign." He didn't stop, "no, no, I've driven in front of that building every morning for as long as I can remember, and this is the first time I've seen your store." I felt like a fool. A cheap fool. I changed conversations as quickly as I could. I was a sorry excuse for an entrepreneur. The next day I crawled down to a student-run marketing club meeting at the nearby college and repented profusely.

SENSEI SAYS

Struggle with life balance, one does, if paid the price to decide what is important, they have not.
- Stephen Covey

Believe me, I've learned my lesson. I can now tell you without the shadow of a doubt that advertising works! I have a lawyer on retainer now because of it. Put together a solid all-encompassing marketing plan and be wise how you spend your money. Don't blithely pass on advertising like I did, just because you think it's an easy expense to limit when you're starting out. Sometimes it's one of the most important expenses you face.

Proverb # 29

There's always another deal around the corner.

f you find yourself entertaining a possible business deal and fear it might fall through, you may feel pressure to sign on the dotted line before you're prepared, or agree to terms that will hurt you in the long run. DON'T! Don't get absorbed into the emotional black hole of thinking there's only one deal out there for you. Once you've done a few deals you realize that they never stop coming. Remember, everyone comes across at least one 'Million Dollar Idea' every 10 years (see Proverb 3). Believe me, if this one goes down in flames, you'll find another one soon enough.

This proverb is applicable across all types of entrepreneurial activity, such as choosing a business partner, loan parameters, insurance policies, funding source, website domain, location, etc. Speaking of choosing a location, when we were ready to open our first store, my wife and I looked at a few different buildings together. I was so anxious to open the doors and get going that I was entertaining retail stores that didn't meet our needs. They just weren't very good. In fact, they were flat-out awful. But I didn't want to lose out if someone came along and gobbled them up, and I needed to get that dang store open. I was about ready to settle on a poor location.

Fortunately, my wife held me back from pulling the trigger until we eventually found an inexpensive, prime location. It sort of just happened. I

RICK•I•PEDIA
The Business Encyclopedia

Traditional IRA

An Individual Retirement Account that allows you to invest up to a certain amount annually with pretax income that grows tax-deferred.

didn't push it or have to make it work out. We didn't have to negotiate through the legalese of some hard-nosed land-lord's lawyer-written lease that was trying to take advantage of

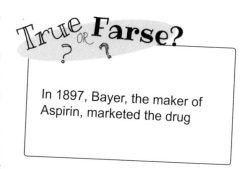

True OR **Farse?**

In 1897, Bayer, the maker of Aspirin, marketed the drug

young entrepreneurs. The storefront just fell in our laps, and we knew it was the right one. This choice, the decision of where to locate our business, has been one of the main keys to our success. If the Truth be told, that one decision may have been the determining fac-tor on whether we'd be in business today or not. When you're choosing locations, always remember, there are more opportunities out there. There is no perfect lo-cation. There are some great locations, and there are many horrendous ones. Be patient. Don't jump the gun. Find the right place for your business to thrive.

Most people say the biggest fear many of us face in life is speaking in public. I don't think that's true. The big-gest fear people face is missing out on an opportunity. A few years back I started to dabble in investment prop-

SENSEI SAYS

Effort fully releases its reward only after quiting, a person refuses to do.
- Napoleon Hill

erty. I had some extra cash that I didn't know what to do with it. We were already do-ing the 401k thing, we'd opened an IRA retirement account, and at Linda's insistence, we'd started fund-ing our kids' education account. These investment tools are all well and good, but I was looking for something more...EXCITING!

Now, let's be honest, the market was downright crappy during the great recession. Real estate had bottomed out and interest rates were so cheap that getting a loan was pretty much borrowing free money. I looked at hundreds of properties, and I'd say nearly 50% of them I was willing to buy. I put low-ball offers down on a lot of them, but many of them came back unaccepted and we moved on. Guess what? That's totally fine. Don't get married to any one deal.

I know, I sound like a grandma talking to her granddaughter about dating. But trust me, there's always more good ones where that came from. There's always another opportunity to take advantage of. And don't worry. The right one will appear, as long as you stick to your principles and keep your eyes open for the truly great deals to come along. Even if Linda and I go out of business due to some future, freakish market-ending scenario , we'll know we gave it our best shot, and that there'll be more ideas to have plenty of fun with coming up after this one.

TRUE

Proverb # 30

You are your own personal brand. How you represent yourself impacts your brand's value.

n my personal life I shop at the Buckle. I like that general look, the collared, relaxed button up, the trendy, stitched ripped jeans, the nice casual vests. At my store I wear that same style of clothes, though sometimes with an athletic edge to it. From a small child I never felt right about dressing up to fit the corporate mold, or to go along with political correctness (PC) in the workplace. In fact, I avoid all things PC so much that I'm actually surprised I haven't faced some kind of workplace HR violation by now…kidding…sort of. My clothing style, haircut, smile, speech, gestures, etc are all part of my personal brand. To me, business casual with jeans represents the new entrepreneur. It's the "I'm too busy creating value for my customers to haul around a suit and tie to every meeting" look. That's me, man! (chuckle) And being true to "me" helps me feel comfortable and ready to go build somethin'.

I was honored with the opportunity to teach entrepreneurship at college after I got my Master's Degree. I felt like the school brought me onto the team because of who I was and what I did. So, I started teaching, wearing my Buckle jeans and Dockers corduroy sport coat. The students re-

RICK·I·PEDIA
The Business Encyclopedia

Personal Branding

The process by which individuals and entrepreneurs differentiate themselves and stand out from a crowd by identifying and articulating their unique value proposition, whether professional or personal, and then leveraging it across platforms with a consistent message and image to achieve a specific goal.

sponded positively to my attire right from the start. They felt like, beyond being about the same age as some, and much younger than others, I was one of 'em. I could relate to their

The "S.O.S" in S.O.S brand scrub pads stands for "Save Our Saucepans."

entrepreneurial dreams and fears. Still today, not a week goes by that I'm not called on by a former student to help him develop his new exciting idea into a vibrant business. Those mentoring sessions have been blessings in my life, opportunities to give back and serve. Helping others...that's why we're here on Earth after all.

After six months of teaching I was invited to be on the business board of advisors to help the school expand entrepreneurship across the entire campus. My job was to show that entrepreneurship is not just for business students, but is truly interdisciplinary. After a quick self-assessment, I decided I would attend the advisor meetings wearing the same attire I lived my life in. It was a risk, but I was going to be true to my personal brand.

I'll never forget how my more casual attire impacted that first of many meetings I was to attend over the next three years. I was surrounded by multiple millionaires dressed to the nines in their business zoot suits. I felt a little out of place to put it mildly. The self-doubt kicked in. Was I wrong to attend a professional meeting underdressed? Was I naïve? I don't know what the right answer is, or if there is a right answer. But one thing's for sure, I was me, and I hoped people would respect that. I forced myself to stand a little taller, smiled big, and started glad handing the other attendees. Randomly, over the next ten minutes I was approached one-on-one by several "Big-Wigs," saying they wished they could dress like me, but felt they had to put on the corporate airs. The stress and worry left as quickly as it had come. I wasn't going to be shamed or ignored. Heck, I was actually going to be envied a little.

I get it, you know, the importance of dressing for the occasion. I'm fine with people representing themselves however they like. I just choose not to apply the corporate business suit requirement to my life. I'm not saying it's right or wrong. I'm sure I burned bridges I never knew about by simply walking in the room wearing jeans. I also know that I opened up many-a-door by being myself and not playing the game straight arrow. You are you, and keeping true to yourself speaks loudly to those around you, for good or ill.

A few months later, I was talking with one of the heads of the university, and she said that she had to enforce a dress code with one of the professors who was wearing jeans to class. I immediately felt a little sheepish, and guiltily admitted, "I wear jeans to teach, too." I knew my face was showing worry. I steeled myself to take a verbal beating like a Catholic school boy reaching his hand out slowly to be smacked with a ruler. To my surprise she quickly replied in a slightly

> **SENSEI SAYS**
> When find yourself on the side of the majority, you do, time it is to pause and reflect.
> - Mark Twain

quieter almost secretive voice, "but you're you, Rick." Then she smiled as if to show me she understood that my actions weren't an act of defiance to stick it to the man. I was just being myself, and she respected that. I felt validated once again in my small actions to stay true to my personal brand. I hadn't put forward a false image. I was who I was, and the powers that be didn't blackball me for it.

Your personal brand is just that, personal. I respect people who know who they are. But don't kid yourself. When you're looking for a job, employers will always check you out and compare you to the other hundred applicants. For instance, I turned down a possible hire once because he was using drugs in pictures on FB. Don't put those pics online. Personally, I'm kind of libertarian on the whole drug-use thing. People can do what they want as long as they're not harming others. But a lady on my HR team saw the Facebook page and loudly asked, "Is that Meth!?! Hey, if he wants to clean the floor with a toothbrush really fast, who cares!"- an act one may pursue while under the influence.

I sort of agreed, but also knew that, as an employer, I have to guard against people who don't show up at work for whatever reason. The online pics struck a nerve with me because I'd actually had an employee once who was on Meth. Now, I was sheltered growing up and didn't know what being on meth looked like. So when my guy came into work high a few times, I didn't recognize the warning signs. My Meth Head employee was a good worker, but he finally dropped the ball by simply not coming in to work. No-call no-show a few times, that kind of thing. Managing him just ended up being tedious.

Here are a few pointers to help you live your brand without adversely affecting future business prospects:

1. Facebook - Keep it clean, smart, and fun, with pics of happy family and friends. You may want to censor the "puking in the toilet" ones.

2. Talents and Hobbies - Be proud and display them...athletics, music, religion, intellect, etc.

3. Sexting - don't do it. (That I have to say this is hilarious...and a little sad!)

4. Tattoos - where, what, and how big are they. People will pre-judge you by your appearance, right or wrong, so think hard before inking.

As an entrepreneur you've got to protect your business because you have employees relying on you for their jobs, your spouse and kids to protect, contracts to fulfill, etc. Like I said earlier, being in business is one thing. Staying in business is another (see Proverb 1).

TRUE

Proverb # 31

Live the "4 Elements of the Entrepreneur."

ervice and entrepreneurship are never going to be about you; they're always centered on the customer. If you can give the customers what they want, you can be reassured they'll come back, and you'll be on your way to making a good chunk of change. The market is much bigger than you. Don't attempt to bend it to your will. When launching a new venture, try to find out what the market needs, and then decide if you can Mentally, Physically, Emotionally, and Financially fill that need. Do you have the "4 Elements of the Entrepreneur?"

Once you've found an under-served market that you believe can sustain a new business entry, you have to decide if you have the stuff to satisfy that demand. This is where the "4 Elements of the Entrepreneur" come in. For you to take on a business in any market, you have to be able to:

1. MENTALLY: Know how to fulfill business procedures, market the product, watch for market changes, guard against shrinkage, and hire good employees. (Or you can try hiring the right professionals to run your business for you, but usually that doesn't turn out well...wink).

2. PHYSICALLY: Retail the product, work early and stay late, walk door-to-door if you

RICK·I·PEDIA
The Business Encyclopedia

Under-Served Market

Products or services inadvertently not provided or under provided for sale, a business opportunity overlooked by a profit-oriented enterprise.

need to boost sales, package and ship orders, and stock the shelves with inventory.

3. EMOTIONALLY: Balance family and work, carry the added stress load, deal with financial loss, and be able to get through a worst case scenario—"full business collapse"—without losing yourself.

4. FINANCIALLY: Know the numbers, price your products well, manage payroll hours, keep good financials, keep the loan money in check, don't over spend on any one section of the business (marketing / rent / benefits / inventory), and most importantly be a good buyer of things.

In a free capitalistic country anyone can succeed if you can supply a demand physically, mentally and financially. There's really no limit to how much money you can make, as long as you can solve someone's problem. This exercise of entrepreneurship is a relatively new model for the world. As I see it, there are two ways to make money...

1. Usurpation

2. Creation

In the dark ages, money was either mined from the earth or stolen from someone else. Under a monarchy, constituents farmed for their livelihood, then were taxed by their liege to pay for costly wars. If they stopped supporting the king they were kicked off the Royal's land. Monarchs would then take the taxes and war with each other for more land, gold, and power. This type of revenue generating is called "usurpation." The term real estate comes from the word "royal-estate," or in other words the king's property. All land fell into this system. Even today we have a similar relationship with government in the

Nearly 60% of all Americans watch TV and surf the Internet simultaneously.

form of real estate taxes. The term "creating money" didn't exist until corporations like the East India Company were formed. These corporations learned that one plus one often can equal a sum greater than that of its parts. From then on creating wealth became a viable (and less bloody) alternative to usurpation.

Much of the world doesn't face the same type of dictatorial rule that our ancestors did. If we can bring value to our community, solve people's problems, and truly help those around us, we can reach financial successes like the world has never known. But again, it all comes back to satisfying the demands of the market. Choose an industry where you can mentally, physically, financially, and emotionally solve problems, and soon you'll be writing your own book with your own life's proverbs of entrepreneurial success. Email me. I'll do your forward.

Proverb # 32

Always have plenty of odor stopper on hand, and never underestimate the power of scent!

e had a $2,000 water vacuum at the store that my wife trusted us with (first mistake). It was the kind of vacuum that used water instead of a bag to collect dirt, so it needed to have the mucky water drained after each use. One day, I went to the back of the store to set it up for some wild vacuuming, and found that it hadn't been drained in a week. It smelled like sewer backup in the office. It was really, really bad! We "Febreezed" the whole store repeatedly, but still didn't come close to solving the odor issue. Customers "noticed" the smell, to put it mildly. That day will go down as one of the worst days in the history of entrepreneurship! Ok, so I'm exaggerating...a little. My store manager couldn't stop dry heaving in the back room. As a kid, I was raised in a 1,000 square foot ranch with six brothers and sisters, so I'm somewhat immune to weird offensive odors. We propped open the doors and "Febreezed" again, this time directly into the carpet. In the end, nothing worked but time. After two days, the scent was gone, but my manager had been scarred for life. He "joked" about that dark day dozens of times over the next few years. Moral of the story: have extra-strength odor remover on hand at your store no matter what.

On another day in the office, I was listening to NPR as a criminologist was being interviewed. The questions posed by the journalist had to do with securing a business against theft and break-ins. Everybody's interested in that, whether by implementing stringent inventory controls, setting up cameras, installing additional locks, bolting down the safe, or carrying a gun. I do most of those things too, but the best crime prevention strategy I've ever heard of came in over the air-

The word "Oral-B" is a combination of oral hygiene and the letter B, which stands for the word "better."

waves that day. The criminologist said that having a good smelling store had as much effect on deterring crime as security cameras. The research concluded that people respond more favorably toward a retail store when they're in a bet-

SENSEI SAYS

Stand adversity all men can. Give a man power and test a man's character it will.
- Abraham Lincoln

ter mood, and scent influences that mood. I was blown away. Who would have thought criminals decided where and when to act based on the amount of potpourri in your store.

The criminal justice professional also noted that the types of magazines you have laying around for customers to read influence criminals' habits. They perceive that if a store lays out magazines that are more sexually focused, that particular store "deserves" to be robbed. I checked my magazine rack and found both Cosmo and Maxim available for perusing. It was a wonder I hadn't been burned down in effigy! I can't tell you if the radio guest's research was valid. I can only say that I immediately canceled my magazine subscriptions and bought a ten year supply of Glade Plug-Ins off eBay.

FARCE = The letter B stands for "brush."

Entrepreneurial
HUMAN RESOURCES

Proverb # 33

Productive thinking is one of the hardest thing to do. That's why it's so profitable.

ne day at the office, my employee Steve mentioned to me that I looked a little lost and distracted. I replied that I was just thinking. He then looked lost himself, like I was speaking in a foreign language. (Not a good sign for long-term employment.) I paused, then said, "you know, Steve, your job is to give great customer service, check prices, clean the store, and organize inventory among many other things. And you do all of this well. My job is different from yours. Yes, I help with all of those things too, working on customer complaints, ordering inventory, setting up our computer system, hiring additional team members, etc. But I also have to come in every day and think of work to assign my employees to do, based on what the store needs to get done. I then have to come up with an implementation plan of how the office is going to accomplish those responsibilities."

I didn't slow down once I was on a roll. Maybe Steve was right. I was a little tightly wound that day. His eyes were glazing over, but I just kept telling him what was on my mind. He brought it up after all! Besides, bilging all of my responsibilities out at Steve kind of helped. "I also have to work with bankers to decide how I am going to get all of this funded. Right now, this month, I'm filing taxes with my accountants, not an easy task. Also, I have

RICK·I·PEDIA
The Business Encyclopedia

Thinking Principle

Constantly thinking of how to improve and efficiently interact with company operations, fellow employees, and customers.

to work on the store expansion contracts and real estate deals we are pursuing."

More employees are injured in the meat packing industry than any other line of work.

Steve was looking more lost with every sentence I laid on him, "I regularly ask myself, do I have enough cash in the bank to close on an investment property, fund growth, buy inventory, or handle payroll? I have to work with my institutional partners and make sure they're taken care of and happy. I watch my wholesalers and distributors and make sure they're paid, but didn't overcharge me. I have to balance family life and church service. And I can't forget to go to the shooting range to blow off some steam. It sounds weird, but maybe I look a little off right now, Steve, because I'm thinking about everything I have to do in the next few days, and planning how I'm going to get it all done." I'm sure he would have been content with an "I'm cool! You?" response, but I wasn't in the mood for general banter right then.

SENSEI SAYS

Educated you are. Certificate, your degree it is. Think of it as a ticket to good life, you may. Ask you to think differently, I will. A ticket to change the world it can be.
- Tom Brokaw

Overall, my employees are well-rounded and entrepreneurial. It's a character trait I look for when hiring. I try to teach the "thinking principle" to my employees regularly, stating that over a lifetime it's the most financially rewarding type of work they can do. Not all of them get it, but most do. I like helping them learn every aspect of the business, and then helping them out personally as well, if I can. We're a family, and I like it that way. But even so, my job is being the entrepreneur, and I am responsible for everything crazy that happens in the store. I have to steer the ship to safe waters—or ships when there are multiple locations involved. As an entrepreneur, you may look haggard sometimes, too, even though you're not. It's just part of the deal. Thinking is tough. Maybe I need an eye-soothing cucumber spa day. Kidding!

Proverb # 34

Hire people through referrals, but hold the referrer honor-bound to vouch for their prospective hire.

llow people to have responsibility for their input into the business' growth. If an employee refers someone, that new hire's work ethic and character reflects directly on the one who referred 'em. One of my lady employees came to me and said, "my boyfriend needs a job. He's a great worker! It'll be so fun working together! I'm sure he'd do great for you here at the store. You should hire him for sure" (Excitable isn't she). She was wearing her heart on her sleeve. I couldn't just say "no."

I thought quickly on how to show appreciation for her finding us someone new to join the team, while not crushing her too badly with the "no couples in the workplace" rule. The solution came to me all at once. To her smiles I replied, "OK, I'll interview him. And let me just tell you: if he works out, it will show great on your recommendation and character. But, if he doesn't do well, it's back on YOU. You have to stand by your referrals, and your honor is on the line." Her mouth gaped a little. She paused and thought about this for a full 2.5 seconds before she looked up at me, excitement squelched out of her, and retorted, "well, I'm not saying he's going to be a great worker. I'm just saying he's available and unemployed and all. You know, if you want to hire him or something. It's your call."

RICK·I·PEDIA
The Business Encyclopedia

Honor-Bound

To be morally held to a high standard of honesty, fairness, or integrity often leading to high public esteem or respect if sustained.

Nearly all of my workers have come through referrals. But I hold the referrers to account on whether the employee does well or not, and they know that,

True or Farse?

The first and longest lasting cartoon characters to promote a Kellogg's product are Snap! Crackle! Pop! from Rice Krispies cereal.

when I talk to them about their contacts in the hunt for great team members. Allowing people to have responsibility for their input into the business's growth has been a huge blessing for me, and has generated thousands of dollars for my stores.

On the other hand, employees don't always have your back, or do what's best for the business. In fact, don't be surprised when a key member of your team up and moves to Kentucky over the weekend, never to return. Trust me, it happens more than you think. One Sunday afternoon, my manager and only employee at one of my distant locations texted me and said that she had moved to, where else, Kentucky over the weekend and was not coming back to work. She and her boyfriend were both getting jobs down there, and she didn't have time to give me two weeks notice, let alone 24 hours. Oh, and she was keeping the cell phone.

SENSEI SAYS

Character, hire you must. Skill, train you can.
- Peter Schutz

I told my wife about the situation we were facing, that I would have to drive to that distant office every day, filling in until I had found a replacement and gotten him up to speed on our procedures. I smiled at her as she openly expressed her frustration about me not being home for the next few weeks (her exact words were too inappropriate to be part of a 'Proverb'). To said outrage I replied, "Linda, that's why we make the big bucks. We have to solve these kinds of problems. That's what entrepreneurs do; they solve problems and create solutions when they're thrown curve balls like this. We'll think and work our way through this, and in a few weeks things will be better than they are today."

Guess what. We applied ourselves, hired an excellent manager, and got the store in order, boosting sales in the process. That's what you have to do as the entrepreneur, think and work your way through obstacles day-by-day. Unfortunately, there will always be another issue over the horizon. In business, you're up to bat every day, and the balls and strikes don't stop comin'. Sometimes you'll strike out, but other times you'll hit it out of the park. Trust me, it's worth the ride.

TRUE

Proverb # 35

Know where you belong.

t college, I double-majored in finance and international business. In one of my many undergraduate finance classes, my teacher/advisor/mentor/dean/professor asked me to join him in a meeting to discuss my future. Before teaching, his background had been in finance. He had opened his own financial brokerage firm back in the day and had brought more than thirty firms through the IPO process—Wealth of knowledge, this guy, especially for a young Finance Major.

I knew my Professor's son had gone to Chicago to work at the Commodities Market, pulling long hours and putting in his time. I was sure that with such dedication he was finding success climbing corporate ladders, getting impressive titles, and following in his dad's footsteps. I respected the work ethic and personal drive, and saw that career path as a plausible option in my life. Also, the possibility of staying in St. Louis to become a Certified Financial Planner (CFP) and pursue employment with Edward Jones or Wells Fargo Financial was on the table. I was an excited young guy, wanting to get out there and make my mark on the world.

After class I met my Professor in his office and he asked me what my goals were after college. He really cared about my future, and obviously wanted to help me make the best decision I could at this pivotal point in my life. I explained the varying career paths I was considering, and that I was leaning toward staying in St. Louis. He frowned a lit-

R$_{ICK}$·$_I$·$_{PED}$$_I$A
The Business Encyclopedia

Initial Public Offering (IPO)

The first sale of stock by a private company to the public. The issuer obtains the assistance of an underwriting firm, which helps it determine what type of security to issue, the best offering price, and the time to bring it to market.

tle, and honestly said that there weren't so many finance opportunities here at home. If I wanted to make a lot of money in finance, I really had to go to a financial hub like Chicago and cut my teeth at

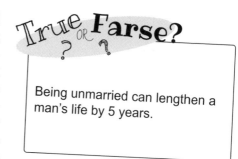

Being unmarried can lengthen a man's life by 5 years.

the Commodities Market like his son was doing. I greatly respected his opinion, and asked him what that job looked like. He said without blinking, " eighty hours a week for 2-3 years to start, sleeping on a cot at the exchange."

Sounds great huh, slaving for years, missing your wife, to die of a heart attack in your 50's. Not to exaggerate too much, but that's kind of how it sounded. After much consideration, I told my mentor my plan. I'd put some numbers together, and with the cost of living increase and my family concerns, I decided that I'd rather stay local, spend time with the kids, make a little less money, and enjoy a lower cost of living, while working 40+ hours a week, not the 80 that he had quoted me. I expected a quick rebuttal like:

1. Life is hard and it's better to get the hard years out of the way when you're young.

2. The world is a bigger place than your home town.

3. Landing an important job right out of college with the right firm can set the foundation for a successful future.

To my surprise he didn't say any of that stuff. Instead he paused, looked at me, smiled with a fatherly twinkle in his eye and said, "Rick, you're wise beyond your years." I knew the respect he had in his heart for his

son's career deci-
sions, but behind
his eyes I could
see the tired effort
that goes into that
lifestyle. Perhaps
he was thinking of
his time on the cot
at the exchange
years earlier. May-
be his daughter-
in-law and grand-
children were on

SENSEI SAYS

When a real
interest in
life you have,
not the most
important thing,
sleep is.
                    - Martha
                        Stewart

his mind. Maybe it was all of it. I couldn't say. One thing
was for sure, though. No matter what direction I went
in life, he knew I'd make it, and that was comforting.

As entrepreneurs we get to decide what types of ventures we're going to pursue, what hours we're going to
put in, what employees we're going to hire, and where
our offices are going to be located. But, if we take ourselves too far away from what's really important, we'll
lose the better part of our lives to money and corporate
success. Let's be honest, that's just glitter. Keep family,
faith, and service big parts of your life, and I promise
you that when you finally leave this Earth you'll have
a smile on your face, knowing that you're leaving it a
better place.

FARCE = Being unmarried can shorten a man's life by 10 years.

Proverb # 36

Form your employee benefits package around your employees' wants and needs, don't simply follow industry averages on compensation.

reat entrepreneurs know how to show their employees they care about them individually and value their personal contributions, and they do it in ways the employees appreciate. When choosing the benefits, you plan to incorporate into your compensation package, for instance, don't simply follow industry averages. Select benefits based on what your employees will use and enjoy. Ask them what they want. Make it a democratic process as much as possible. At my office we voted on where to have our business meeting, and the consensus was we'd have a Trampoline Dodgeball day, then head to Busch Stadium for a Cardinals baseball game! How much business did we get done at the so called "business meeting?" As much as we needed to... (wink).

I don't think the standard model of "corporate benefits" applies as directly to our lives today as it did, say 25 years ago. Our Interests, needs, and lives in general have changed. People want to receive benefits in a way that's more personal than bureaucratic. . If you think about the person and their interests and what they're going through in their life and tailor you compensation to mirror their needs, your benefits package is going to be much more impactful.

Employee benefits are kind of like birthday presents, in that they can be personalized to suit your employees' lifestyles and

RICK•I•PEDIA
The Business Encyclopedia

Bureaucratic

Rigid, procedural, structural, official, unadaptable, administrative, governmental.

PERSONALIZED BENEFITS

- Baseball Games
- Rock Concerts
- Salon Gift Cards
- Collectible Comics
- Shooting Days at the Gun Range
- Free Lunch Everyday
- Ultimate Frisbee
- Free Use of Intl. Timeshare
- Hockey Games
- Entertaining Business Meetings

TRADITIONAL BENEFITS

- 10% Annual Raises
- 401-k Program
- Corporate Training Trips
- Cell Phones for Managers
- Gym Memberships
- Lax Time-off Program

interests. In my business we have two types of benefits. We call them "Personalized Benefits" and "Traditional Benefits". My team loves it. I love it. Having part of your benefits program open to personalization

True OR Farse?

The reason the Animal Crackers box is designed with a string handle is because when the popular circus theme was introduced in 1902 they thought the crackers would also be purchased as Christmas novelties and hung from Christmas trees.

is fun for everyone involved, and we grow closer through the process. I'm not telling you to completely walk away from the traditional benefits packages found in Corporate America. I'm

SENSEI SAYS

Get people to do what you want them to do, because want to do it, they do. True motivation, this is.
- Dwight D. Eisenhower

just saying that, while you're putting your compensation structure together, try to build it around your people. It's for them after all.

BEST BUSINESS MEETING EVER!

WORLD SERIES

Proverb # 37

Strive to make the terms of any deal a win-win for everyone.

'm painfully blunt with people, have been since I was a kid. I don't keep secrets or play games. I call it like I see it and put all my cards on the table. (I'd make a horrible politician) When hiring for a new position at my office, I don't lowball people just to see what I can get out of them. I try to make every deal I make a win-win all around, whether it's a building lease, employee salary, professional contract services, etc. I don't believe in win-lose deals. They don't exist in my world. If it's not a win-win, it's a lose-lose all around. No exceptions.

A few years back I noticed some picketers outside a major grocery chain in my town. I walked up to them and asked why they were picketing. They cheered almost in song, "for our quarter raise!" They then added, "the CEO and board of directors make way too much money." That was pretty much the extent of their argument. They handed me some basic reading material and felt like the debate was over.

I really should have moved on at that point, but I really wanted to know about the issue, so I started to play devil's advocate in hopes of getting to the root of the problem. "Well," I said, "if the CEO and board of directors make no money at all, you'll probably get a quarter raise across all the employees in the company. But then many of the board members would quit, leaving you without quality leadership and direction." They didn't accept my premise, or even seem to care. I went on to explain how grocery stores live on a 2% profit margin, and that the local

$R_{ICK} \cdot I \cdot PEDI_A$
The Business Encyclopedia

Win-Win
Entering contracts or resolving conflicts where all participants gain and are satisfied. Contrary to a Zero-Sum game where there is always a winner and a loser.

newspaper had just reported that, if the strike went on for 4 more weeks, the grocer would literally go out of business due to lack of revenue. If that happened, their jobs would be gone, and Wal-Mart or

True OR Farse?

All lottery winners lose their winnings in about 2 years.

some other non-union shop would take over the grocery section of the town, leaving their union forever weakened and them looking for work.

No dice. The picketers went back to chanting. It was they vs. management, and they knew in their core they were right on this. It seemed to me like these unions were cannibalizing their own jobs. But to each his own. I went back home and followed the story's progression over the next few days on the radio and TV. It was reported that the costs of the health insurance the grocers were providing to their employees had spiked over the previous few years (we all know about that). To cover the higher insurance costs the grocer had to refuse the quarter raise.

Two weeks later, as the grocers were about to file bankruptcy, with bankers breathing down their necks, the unions agreed to go with a contract that looked very similar to the one the grocer had offered months earlier. In the end it was much ado about nothing, and it

SENSEI SAYS

Why want to win, do I? Because want to lose, I do not!

– Max Schmelling

cost the employees and the grocer a lot of money in lost revenue. When everyone signed and shook hands, crowds immediately formed at the stores across the county and began buying up all the goods they'd done without for the last few months. The whole deal was a lose-lose-lose all around.

In our days on this Earth, all of us will change our occupational hats several times, as opportunities swerve and bounce us through life. As entrepreneurs and managers, we need to help our employees feel like they have a stake in the business. They need to feel like they're partners with management in the success of the company. It's our job to create a healthy enjoyable company culture where all are part of a family, valued and rewarded for jobs well done, and consistently offered opportunities for advancement and personal development.

As employees, we need to understand the needs of the business we work under. If we aren't making the company stronger, we're making it weaker. Be proud of what you build, what your labor produces. Perform a full day's work for a full day's wage. We're all in this life together. Let's make all of our endeavors win-win for everyone no matter what side of the table we're sitting on.

FARCE = While most of them do lose their money quickly, all of them gain weight.

Proverb # 38

Understand 'Maslow's Hierarchy of Needs' pyramid, and know which rung you're on.

aslow is applicable to almost anything, including all sections of your "Entrepreneur's Bible". I know, I think of the word "marshmallow" every time I see his name too. But oh well! Stay with me. Here's a general definition of the pyramid:

Maslow's Hierarchy of Needs is a multi-runged pyramid of needs and motivations. The bottom rung begins with basic physiological needs such as water, food, clothing, shelter. Going from the bottom up, once we've satisfied the needs of a particular rung we are free to attempt to satisfy the needs on the rung above until we reach the pinnacle "self-actualization."

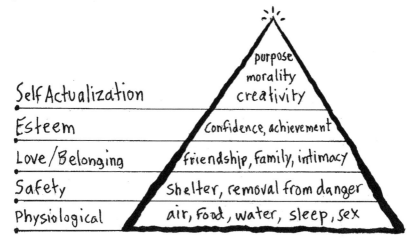

It's an important duty to understand this pyramid, and know which rung you're on at all times as you may fluctuate up or down the pyramid randomly through life. To break it down, you've got to be satisfied in your basic needs before you can move on to a higher form of satisfaction in your life. Don't take on the question marks of entrepreneurship and small business until you're at least working on the second rung. I'll go further and say that a great entrepreneur also knows where his employees are on the Hierarchy of Needs pyramid and consistently helps them advance up the ladder to success.

I had a friend in college who left Maslow's advice in the classroom and turned the pyramid upside down. He wanted all the financial rewards and emotional benefits that come with entrepreneurial success before he took care of his basic needs...you know,

SENSEI SAYS

If succeed, you will, find something to motivate and inspire, you must.
- Tony Dorsett

food, shelter, etc. In his haste to "make it happen," he ended up dropping out of college, living out of his car, and straining familial relationships. These consequences inadvertently stunted the growth of his business. He wasn't physiologically secure, so he couldn't dedicate his undivided attention to entrepreneurial development. In the end, he finally turned Maslow back upright, got control of his life, and took care of his immediate living conditions. He got married, had a kid, and opened a new business with great contracts in place.

He's a true success story. Yes, he fell a few times getting off the line, but who doesn't! We all make mistakes and fall short sometimes. It's the getting back up and trying again down the hard road that defines us. I try to live by Maslow in my marriage, entrepreneurial endeavors, investments, and social engagements. I think eventually we all have to.

Entrepreneurial
OPERATIONS

Proverb # 39

Successful businesses often have to pivot 3 times before making any real money.

I audited a business plan competition a few years ago when I was building the Duree Center for Entrepreneurship. I wanted to find out what other schools and centers were doing and recreate what worked. It's always good to check out the competition. I spoke to some of the venture capitalists (VC's) who were there judging the business ideas. One of them opened up to me, explaining that his firm invested in up to 20 businesses at a time. Over the years, they had invested in 10 different businesses from that particular competition. Of course, he passed on hundreds of investment opportunities and selected the top ten he felt his firm could help and profit from.

I asked him which of those ten ideas were the best, and he said it wasn't about the ideas, it was about the people. "We're investing 80% in the people, 20% in the business," he said, "because every business pivots at least 3 times before it breaks out." I asked him how his ten investments had done. He said six of them had lost money and were going out of business, three of them had done well enough to break even, and only one of them had exploded, scaling up nationally for huge profits for the firm.

Through his years of investing in businesses, he

RICK·I·PEDIA
The Business Encyclopedia

Pivoting

Keeping one foot of your business model firmly in place as you shift the other in a new direction. In this way, new ventures process what they have already learned from past success and failure and apply these insights in new areas.

had learned that on average every new venture pivots, or changes focus, at least three times before breaking out and becoming profitable. The ones that can't

Two-thirds of small businesses change the content on their website less frequently than once a month.

stick and move with the market go out of business and are forgotten. The people who entrepreneurially guide their businesses into new markets or adapt their "Entrepreneur's Bible" to follow a different and innovative model often succeed wildly. Let's be honest. Your path to success will probably take some time, whether your initial idea takes hold or not. The goal is always to truly satisfy demand. If you don't, you're gonna lose.

Many venture capital firms are forming regional Accelerators, facilities dedicated to fostering entrepreneurial collaboration and creativity, and infusing that energy with capital to accelerate growth. Their end goals often include an exit strategy of selling the incubated businesses to strategic multinational corporations at some

SENSEI SAYS

Searches, responds, and exploits change, an entrepreneur does.

- Peter F. Drucker

future date. Over the last ten years, a large swatch of these VC's have focused on tech businesses that don't carry inventory or massive and payrolls, thus limiting warehousing and retail store overhead.

Ben and Jerry's was originally going to be a bagel company.

Today, the venture capital market is changing somewhat. After so many failed tech companies have fallen to the wayside, unable to generate profits for themselves or their investors, many VC's are starting to look for businesses that already have some revenues from existing customers prior to investing. This limits different risks investors take on. Yes, there are inventory and staff to take care of, but there are revenues as well. Can you imagine? Bootstrapping to produce a viable product, and then selling it to eager buyers for a profit...who would have thought! I guess the old ways of doing business are still true today.

Proverb # 40

Your business is your business. You share the successes with your team, but own the mistakes yourself.

built the warehouse side of my business for the first three years I was open, running it primarily myself. It was fairly easy to operate, but everyone knows mundane warehouse work can get old. Being honest, after three years I just didn't want to do it anymore, so I hired someone else to man the facilities. Right off, the people I hired did a pretty good job running things without me. On the other hand, because I wasn't there I unfortunately didn't take the time to give these new hires continued procedural oversight or regular praise for their efforts. I had separated myself from that section of the business, trusting in my manager and staff to operate the department. Shockingly, and without much warning, the main wholesaler working with our warehouse dropped us like a rock a year after I left my duties there. The wholesaler cited customer relations issues as the reason for kicking us to the curb. Even though I repeatedly appealed the charges in length, they never looked back. As I saw it, this was an unfair decision by the wholesaler, and ended up being a lose-lose for all involved.

As an entrepreneur, you have to deal with what comes your way, both the good and the disturbingly bad. My team and I took a month to research what had gone wrong, reorganized, and fixed the problem quickly and effective-

RICK·I·PEDIA
The Business Encyclopedia

Wholesaler

Someone other than your standard customer who buys from you in bulk at a discount and resells the products to other businesses.

ly. Unfortunately, we had to let some people go. During the next round of hiring, I made it my personal goal to instill in the new team members the importance of

True or Farse?

40% of McDonald's profits come from the sales of Happy Meals.

customer service and being detail-oriented.

It was the early summer when we needed revenue from the wholesaler the most. We needed to make payroll, and I had been counting on those sales. I had to finagle and hustle to get cash for the bills. I did what I had to do, went through cash advances on all my credit cards and opened additional lines of credit with two banks. I considered approaching friends for short-term loans, but family poned up some dough first. Not the best situation to find myself in, but we got through it.

In the end we got it worked out, but that was a turning point in my life entrepreneurially. Never again would I be caught like that, so financially naked before the

SENSEI SAYS

Serious mistakes we face. Not because wrong answers we receive but from the wrong questions we ask.
- Peter F. Drucker

world. Those five weeks of worry, wondering where the money was going to come from, represent a little piece of Hell I'll never forget. All that fear and anguish could have been avoided.

Your business is your business. You share the successes with your team all day long, but own the mistakes yourself and solve those problems. That may not sound fair, but get used to it. Entrepreneurs are problem solvers. Keep your eyes on your business, because it's always better not to have mistakes in the first place, then have to fix them afterward.

Proverb # 41

When writing a
contract, make it a
win-win deal for
all involved.

n signing the contract for my fourth university bookstore location, I was really going out on a limb on my costs. I was trying my darndest to give the students and the school the best deal I could. Being honest, though, I didn't know if I was going to lose my shirt and be $100,000 in the hole at the end of the first year. One thing I did know, however, was that I was going into business with some very honest partners who wanted our deal to be a win-win-win all around. I knew that if I tried my hardest to be a team player, keep my prices down, and share in the labor, marketing, and infrastructure costs, then, if push came to shove, my new partners would come through and finesse our deal so that no one lost.

This is a scary place to be in business. Sometimes putting yourself and your business in hard financial situations is necessary to solidify a deal. Just look at the big box stores' suppliers who are really squeezed to get their prices down. Believe me, you never want to be in those situations with people you don't trust.

Close your eyes and imagine what's happening behind the scenes at company headquarters. People you don't see at the reception counter are writing up the leases, mortgages, car notes, etc. These contracts are all put together the same way. . A contracts person

---

RICK·I·PEDIA
The Business Encyclopedia

Four Corners

A contract that appears complete on its face is to be represented by the words on the page only, and no outside evidence may be considered.

creates the document and hands it off to the sales rep who retains some maneuverability with the terms, so as to not lose the deal. Therefore, the terms are al-

True or Farse?

The Rams were the first U.S. football team to introduce emblems on their helmets.

most always adjustable. Read every contract thoroughly and add clauses or change phraseology, so it reads in your favor. Why the heck not! Negotiation is part of making deals. Sometimes people will surprise you and just say 'sure' to whatever you add to the inter-business contract, so write in as many safety clauses as you can think of. If you don't get your amendments, but still want to do the deal, at least you've shown that you won't be easily pushed around. Just as in sports, business is a mental game. How you portray yourself is how you'll be treated.

Yes, when wise old Anonymous said, "everything is negotiable," he meant it. But in the end you have a responsibility to make sure it's still a win-win deal for all.

SENSEI SAYS

The government, a senior partner it is, in every business in the country.
– Norman Cousins

Think about it, if the people you're working with are willing to bend over backwards for you, just like you are for them, some of the fear that comes along with depending on others can be eliminated through trust. Full disclosure: not all entrepreneurs will agree with me here. The "Four Corners" rule is a foundational principle for some people. Maybe I'm not following the rules of "Business Deals 101," but for me, I have to have some level of trust in people I am working with. In my life, faith doesn't stop at church. Have faith in the right people. It's good for your business, and it's good for your soul.

Proverb # 42

Insurance companies don't do well with verbal contracts. I know, I've tried.

re you ready for an insurance horror story? First let me say,"my name is Rick Duree and I'm a high maintenance client." There, I feel better now that that's out there. Most entrepreneurs need strong team members to keep them sharp. When I recruit a lawyer, financial advisor, or accountant I tell them I need them to be in my business with me, not just an external source of legal and tax filings. Once you open multiple store locations, hold large amounts of inventory, and have to get life insurance to insure business loans against your untimely demise, you'll understand why entrepreneurs simply want to pass all insurance responsibilities off to their trusted hardworking agent.

Originally, my business was located in two separate buildings. It wasn't efficient, but it was cheaper than the alternative at the time. One day, I called my insurance guy and told him I was building out my main store. I was moving out of the satellite location that month and consolidating all my business into the main office. I explained that I wanted to increase my insurance coverage at the main store to satisfy the transfer in of inventory from the satellite location. Naturally, I asked him to drop the insurance coverage on the satellite location immediately. He quickly increased my rates at my main store and we got the policy hike intact. Everything

---

RICK·I·PEDIA
The Business Encyclopedia

Consolidate

To combine into a more effective, solidified, or coherent unit or system.

looked good. Normal business procedures, right?

One year later I received a letter from an insurance company stating that my old satellite office's insur-

True or **Farse?**

The highest denomination ever minted by the U.S. Treasury was the $1,000 bill, the lowest was the $1 bill.

ance policy would be lapsing soon and they wanted me to renew it in the coming months. What? The insurance from my old satellite location had not yet been canceled? I was blown away and called my insurance guy immediately. I asked him what was going on. I said that I thought we had canceled the satellite policy and increased the insurance on my main store the year before. So, why was I getting a bill? Had the insurance company been drafting my checking account without authorization that whole year? He calmly replied, "well, you needed to give the cancellation to me in writing." I couldn't believe it. I hadn't given him the insurance increase in writing. Where were these paperwork requirements coming from?

SENSEI SAYS

Do your best to your utmost ability, your purpose it is. Have high standards I do.
- Donald Trump

I concluded that my team member had let me down. He might have made a mistake, and wasn't going to own up to it. He said there was nothing we could do. No refund for that unused, unrequested insurance was going to be issued simply because I hadn't sent him an email when we spoke the year earlier. I had just called him on the phone about the cancellation, and apparently that wasn't enough. Then belligerently he cut at me through the phone, "you're the one paying the bills. You should know what your policies are. You should know what you're paying for." (click!) In utter shock I found myself listening to dial tone. True story.

In the end we got coverage in no time. I was referred to a new agent and had a new policy in place before the week was out. I saved a good chunk of money, too! I don't expect you to know insurance policy. I don't know insurance jazz myself! I just buy whatever they sell me that seems to fit within my model. That's what insurance people are there for. That's why they get paid. If you haven't experienced crappy professional service in your business life yet, prepare for it to slither your way sometime in the future. After it happens, you'll watch your hired professionals closer, and try never to let it happen again because it sucks! Remember that.

FARCE = The highest denomination ever minted by the U.S. Treasury was the $100,000 bill, the lowest was the 5 cent bill.

Proverb # 43

Efficiency
vs. Effectiveness.
(efficient is not
always effective)

y strict definition:

EFFICIENCY: functioning at peak performance with the least waste of time and effort.

EFFECTIVENESS: ability to produce the desired result.

You need to be efficient in areas that increase sales and expand your business. Or, in other words, spend your valuable resources to make more money. Functioning at peak performance in areas that don't directly grow your bottom line, however, may be a waste of time and money. If you're efficient in areas that count, you're being effective, hopefully producing a cash result.

Be careful here. If you instill internal bureaucracy in your team several manuals deep to limit human error, and use up large amounts of labor, capital, and planning time in order to achieve the peak performance you're looking for, your über-efficient procedures may have just bogged you down, setting the business back financially. Don't completely neglect peak performance. It's always the goal. Just don't choose it over financial stability. This is hard for perfectionists and new entrepreneurs.

We find this type of imbalance a lot in big business. Excessive managerial requirements and paperwork forced on department heads and intrapreneurs by vice presidents who think they know best often yield inefficient outcomes. This happens mostly because VP's can become separated from the hand-on

RICK·I·PEDIA
The Business Encyclopedia

Business Board Advisor

Someone outside the business who is invited to idea generating meetings to give critical evaluations of the business and help it grow.

running of the day-to-day operations, hindering the ability to directly customize company needs to a the aptitudes of a specific department. In other words, you can see the game best if you're close

True or Farse?

The Code of Federal Regulations makes it illegal for U.S. citizens to have any contact with extraterrestrials or their vehicles.

to the action. Not surprisingly, the bureaucracy never lessens. It only becomes thicker over time. Don't go down this path with your own internal bureaucracy. Be efficient when it counts, but don't drown yourself in paperwork or go crazy micro-managing your team. That wouldn't be effective.

Efficiency and effectiveness don't stop with bureaucratic procedures. Suppliers, for instance, will remember you out of a crowd of retailers, if you treat them fairly and pay them promptly. Want to build a reputation for being an effective business person? Simply pay your bills on time. That's one area of entrepreneurship you should become very efficient at. It's not too hard, and your reputation as a responsible party will grow fast. These suppliers may ask you out of the blue to be on their business board of advisors, or join with them on a cross-business marketing campaign, just because you impressed them in doing what you said you would do. Be efficient in paying your invoices on time and you'll stand out from the crowd. Now, that's effective.

SENSEI SAYS

The hand of government, slow and heavy it is. The invisible hand of the market, better and faster it moves.
— Mitt Romney

My bank asked me to be on their board of advisors

in my second year of business. Then, in my fourth year, my main supplier invited me to be on their business board of advisors. There were several reasons why these opportunities came my way, but one of them most definitely was that I did what I said I was going to do.

- Honor
- Integrity
- Follow Through

These character traits are less common than you might think. Business people recognize and appreciate them right out of the box, because they're less common than one might think. Simply by seeing me live these principles, my business contacts gained confidence in my entrepreneurial skill set, and increased faith that I could be a financially stable partner.

If you are efficient and effective in all aspects of your life, whether professional or personal, you're going to win over your suppliers, beat your competitors, gain new customers, and be in business a very long time. That last sentence may sound like the self-fulfilling John Madden line, "usually the team with the most points wins the game!" But guess what: usually the team with the most points wins the game. I hope you can priori-tize the important things in life, keeping a good balance between efficiency and effectiveness.

IS THAT A VOLCANO OR A MOUNTAIN, AYE?

YES.

VOLCANOS ARE ALWAYS MOUNTAINS, BUT MOUNTAINS AREN'T ALWAYS VOLCANOS.

TRUE

Proverb # 44

When working B2B, try to understand the other company's needs, and build your partnership to be mutually beneficial.

teach Entrepreneurship at college, and not a week goes by that I don't get a call from an excited entrepreneur asking for help in getting their new venture successfully launched. I'm honored to be seen as someone who may be able to help. But to give quality advice to my students and others, I need to understand intimately their visions for the future companies. This lesson was taught to me by the man who embodies this proverb more than anyone else I've ever known, Dustin, my first banker. He took a risk with me and my new startup. That act alone was gracious enough, but what really set him apart from other service professionals was the attention he gave me as I was getting started out there in world.

Over my first few years, Dustin would come to my store once a month with ideas he had thought up to help grow my business. This commitment to my entrepreneurial success went far in telling me what kind of man he was. I suppose that, as my banker, he felt a kind of stewardship over my store, longing for it to get off the ground and grow. I've noticed, however, that most bankers don't have that partnership personality. He was definitely on my team. His actions proved that loyalty.

Because of the relationship he fostered with me, I went to him first with all my future bank-

RICK·I·PEDIA
The Business Encyclopedia

Business to Business (B2B)

Commercial transactions between businesses, often between people who know and trust one another.

ing business, including home loans, auto loans, credit cards, and other lines of credit. I also strongly referred him to several of my friends. When working business to business (B2B), both companies have to walk together toward a mutually beneficial goal. You must become deeply involved in the other company's needs and processes in order to provide them with real solutions to their problems.

True or Farse?

On average a business document is copied 10 times.

Unfortunately, Dustin ended up leaving the bank where I had met him and moving out of state. It seems silly writing it, but I cried a little that day. A mentor was retiring from my team, and he was going to leave a big hole. Happily, the lending continued between my store and that small town bank, and the new loan officer tried his best to fill Dustin's shoes. But it was never the same. I still call Dustin for advice on business development and keep him up to date on my company's growth because I know he'll take it seriously and put his all into helping me expand. He really cares, down to his soul. Do you have that kind of charity? Fostering those kind of relation-

SENSEI SAYS

Involving and fun, a business, must be. Exercise your creative instincts, it should.
— Richard Branson

ships is what B2B is all about, and what great entrepreneurs and teammates do all the days of their lives.

I'm not gonna lie to you. Being brave and engaged with your business can be hard. You have to trust in your product/service, your B2B partners, and most importantly yourself. As the entrepreneur, you have the most intimate relationship with your business. Often, you have to feel your way through the haze of sales predictions and advertising tactics. Your instincts can be more accurate and market penetrating than a consultant's when it comes to knowing your customers. Be absolutely open-minded to advise, but know that you are the creator, the thinker, and are ultimately responsible for the success of your business.

Proverb # 45

It's hard to teach old dogs new tricks if they never stop doing the old tricks.

any department stores are open 24/7, selling just about anything you can think of for great prices. Why do we keep going back for more department store sales, you might ask? Well, we don't go back because the stockers and checkers are exceptional salespeople. And we definitely don't keep going to check out all the beautiful people. (There are tons of YouTube videos proving that). No, the truth is we keep going back to department stores because the business model they've built has such a strong foundation. The supply chain is what makes the money.

When you buy a product at any of the main department stores across the country, their point of sale computer marks that inventory decrease, and immediately places an order for another one of those same products from a centralized distribution center. The whole process takes seconds. Fleets of 18-wheelers then load up the newly ordered products at massive docking bays and drive day and night, rushing to your hometown store to keep the shelves stocked for the next customer. Think about it, have you ever gone to a department store and found them out of something? Be honest, it's rare. Their system keeps the trucks moving and your shopping cart full. It's a brilliant entrepreneurial

RICK·I·PEDIA
The Business Encyclopedia

Supply Chain

System of product management that includes all steps of production, shipping, wholesaling, and retailing to bring a product to the end consumer.

masterpiece of effi-
ciency.

According to research, the least productive workday is Monday and the most productive is Wednesday.

In business, you have to strive for efficien-cies throughout all sections of your com-pany, or the competi-tion will eat you alive.

Years ago GM and Toyota teamed up to share technol-ogy and business procedures. Toyota hoped to learn more about doing business in America, while one of GM's goals was to try to imitate Toyota's efficiencies. Both companies had a learning curve, but GM especial-ly ran into some issues. First, Toyota told GM to close each of its plants down for 3 months, freeing up the floor to bring in new machinery and other upgrades. GM's unions didn't want their workers to lose pay for three months, so they fought to keep the plants open while they upgraded. Well, as you might have guessed, it's hard to teach your employees new procedures with new equipment, if they're still using their old tech-niques daily, on obsolete machinery. Also, the setup of the new machines was slowed when the plant was still pumping out cars regularly. In other words, it's hard to teach old dogs new tricks, if they never stop doing the old tricks.

Second, Toyota told GM they needed to let go 25% of their work force, because the new machines they had brought in had ultimately replaced some of their line workers. Well, neither GM, nor the unions wanted that fight, so a negotiation was quickly reached where some employees were laid off, but not nearly the number

Toyota recommended. Then, Toyota told GM to put its people in groups, and upgrade the person to person assembly line system used by manufacturers to build cars since Henry Ford was alive. Going forward, GM was to build cars group to group.

The goal of this the new group-focused assembly line was to have everyone on the team exchange jobs occasionally, switching responsibilities so they would know how to do all the different tasks their team was in charge of. Employees' skills would increase and the monotony of working on the line would diminish. If someone was sick, the team could easily cover for their partner. If someone's arm was tired from a strenuous procedure, they could switch with another worker and share the load.

According to Toyota, a group-focused assembly line would increase company-wide productivity along with profits. It sounded like a win-win for labor and management. Not so fast! The unions didn't like the new group focus because, if the group had a weak link slowing down production, the whole team would lose out on bonuses, or face other disciplinary actions. If someone was screwing around or coming to work drunk, the group members would be pressured to tell management which group member

SENSEI SAYS

The difference between revenue and expense, profit is. Remind people of this. Make you look smart, it will.
– Scott Adams

was either under performing or under qualified. No union member wanted to be responsible for another worker getting reassigned, or worse.

Needless to say, Toyota's group-focused assembly line recommendation has been difficult to implement. There's a GM plant in my town, and I know a team leader from one of these groups personally. The peer pressure to under perform or turn your head if someone isn't pulling their own weight is intense. GM is a great company, but they need to really work on their company culture if any new efficiencies are to be achieved in the near future.

In this case study, we can see how GM's team of managers and employees were unable to stop performing their old tricks long enough to become competitive. Eventually, bankruptcy slammed them in the face when the Great Recession hit, and a lot of new tricks were forced on the historic car manufacturer. You never want to be pushed into company-wide restructuring. When you find inefficiencies, adopt new procedures yourself, before the "Invisible Hand" (see Proverb 5) forces you into a corner and spanks your butt.

FARCE = The least productive workday is Friday and the most productive is Tuesday.

Entrepreneurial
EXPANSION

Proverb # 46

You need a 5-year plan every day of your life.

etting goals is a constant in every successful entrepreneur's life. Always have a 5-year plan guiding your efforts to insure your individual and professional progression continues. To accomplish your 5-year master vision, you need to set more attainable 3-year goals, built on three defined 1-year milestones, to help get you there. Have several shorter-term steps you can accomplish relatively quickly to help yourself mentally and emotionally get to your major 3 and 5-year goals. You'll find yourself making big steps in your life and realizing bits of the satisfaction you are reaching for.

Tangential mini-plans, that seem to just pop up as you're working through your yearly goals, and end up getting added to your life along the way, are totally accepted, even encouraged. They keep your eyes open to new ideas and help you stay interested in life, as you're on your way to true success. I've had a 5-year plan since I was 12 years old, and it's done well for me, but it evolved as I grew and my priorities changed. I've been strengthened by the journey, always being encouraged and even pushed by my ambition to keep going.

There was a low time in my life when I only had a 1-year plan in effect. I was turning 30 and had accomplished all my goals up to that point in my life. That mindset I had, that most of my goals were accomplished at 30, was actually pretty childish and naive. I wasn't thinking big enough. I was ignoring the "Thinking Principle" I teach my employees and students daily (see Proverb 33). Everything I had

Rɪᴄᴋ·ɪ·ᴘᴇᴅɪA
The Business Encyclopedia

Tangent

A digression toward a different thought or action that takes attention away from the original focus or goal.

accomplished to that point was just the tip of the iceberg of what life had to offer. I couldn't see it, though, because my vision wasn't mature enough. I thought I'd end up drifting

True OR **Farse?**

The founder of FedEx once saved the company by taking its last $5,000 and turning it into $32,000 by gambling in Vegas.

through life after that last 12 months expired. But that's the ironic beauty of always working toward a better tomorrow, you get there eventually. After that you have to find new inspiration to drive you on.

Another "Dreamer's" story presented itself to me when I was 16 years old and working at Dairy Queen. A 17-year-old girl came up to me on break and said, "Rick, what kind of house do you want when you get older?" I thought to myself, "I'm 16! I'm a guy. I don't care about houses. What the heck is this girl talking about?" But, I decided to play along. I looked at her and said, "I don't know, a two-story I guess? With a garage? I don't know. What about you?" She smiled at the opportunity to divulge her adult visions to me; "you know...those double-wide mobile homes are looking really nice these days." (True story!) I was blown away! I had a lot of buddies who lived in trailer parks, and it's whatever, do what you want to do. But if you're asking me about your grand future home goals, you probably don't finish with a double-wide. Just sayin'.

SENSEI SAYS

Do everything we can, we must, to make entrepreneurial dreams a reality.
- Ross Perot

I asked my dad later that night what he thought about

this whole conversation because I didn't know where to go with it. As always, he said something insightful: "it's easy to understand her, Rick. People judge something on how they would deal with it. People build their life based on what they've seen and experienced." I said, "yeah, you're right. She lives in a trailer right now with her family." And he says to me, "that's what she knows. And it is what it is, not right or wrong." That, my friends, is a truism, a life-lesson. I had met all my goals at 30 because I wasn't thinking big enough. I hadn't experienced enough of life to know what other options were available to me. The world out there is global, and I was thinking local small town. I thought I'd end up drifting through life after the next 12 months expired because I had met all my goals up to the point. But, like I said, that's the beauty of always working toward your goals... you will accomplish them eventually, and then you have to find new ones to strive for.

We need to dream at a macro level with a grand wish list for ourselves, families, and communities. We can accomplish anything if we just keep striving toward it. I know that sounds Utopian, but it's true in so many ways, in so many people's lives, that we cannot deny it.

Proverb # 47

Don't be afraid of giving up partial ownership in your business in exchange for long term stability and growth.

enture Capitalists (VC's) are in business because they've succeeded in funding profitable business ventures in the past. Having a Venture Capitalist on your side will go far in developing your business beyond the limits you can currently see. You'll have the cash to do the product development and expansion you need to launch to the next level quickly. There will come a time in your entrepreneurial life when you won't be able to make all the money yourself. You'll need equity partners, and they'll have a say in the development of your business and share in the profits. Sometimes you have to compromise to get the deal done and move forward.

Venture Capitalists face financial pressures like all of us. If they lose too much of their money, they're out of the lending business, just like a bank. Because of this financial risk they take on with each deal they pursue, going in to meet one can be a little weird. You may never experience this level of business scrutiny again. Watch reruns from ABC's venture capitalist reality TV show "Shark Tank" to get a good grasp of how VC's talk, what's important to an investor when he's deciding to put up his money, what his physical movements may tell you about what he's thinking, and the way the meeting may go. I'll tell you right

Rick·i·pedia
The Business Encyclopedia

Venture Capital

Professional investors pool together their millions of dollars and invest in early stage entrepreneurial ventures with the desire to grow the companies rapidly and usually sell them off in under five years for a large return.

now, they're going to ask for equity in your business up front in exchange for their money, contacts, and management advice. Be prepared for an onslaught of probing, possibly uncomfortable questions. You need to:

1. Have a preset limit of how much control you'll give the investor in exchange for cash.

2. Know your market.

3. Know your financials. Know your product.

4. Basically, know everything...(wink)

For some VC's, investing in startups is their hobby. They will try to exploit your financial need for their equity gain. It's the name of the game. They'll push you to lower your equity valuation down to their advantage. I don't play games like this, verbally devaluing companies

SENSEI SAYS

Capital, scarce it is not. Vision, hard to find it is.
– Sam Walton

and sound financial projections to take advantage of someone in real financial hurt. But come on now. Don't take it too personally. VC's are called sharks for a reason. If you're gonna fight them in their octagon, you're gonna have to get used to taking hits. Take these "Proverbs of Profit" to heart and use them as your entrepreneurial Jiu-Jitsu in battle.

Venture Capitalists are serious people and want to work with serious partners. Investors want to be able to trust tha,t when they lean on you for something, it will get done. Life doesn't have to become stale, full of work and stress and deadlines. Having fun is a must. You have to enjoy what you're doing for you to find fulfillment in your entrepreneurial journey. But when it's time to get down to business, keep smiling and recognize that the games have to be put on pause. Other businesses will rely heavily on you to fulfill contracts and do your job. Don't crack under the stress. If you can't deliver, or if you come across as too superficial or distracted, they're not going to take you seriously, and you're going to lose a B2B partner.

Equity investors can be great assets and long-term team members, connecting you to a wealth of important people and ideas. They answer questions you never knew to ask and open doors you never knew were there. Go into these meetings with your eyes open. VC's can help you... if you don't lose your shirt in the process... (wink)

TRUE

Proverb # 48

You can't be everything to everybody, so focus on being great at what you do well!

I opened up my first college bookstore with 12 textbooks laid out randomly across 24 shelf units. Not exactly a full inventory. When a journalist came by to write an article on the new book-store in town, we threw all the books onto one shelf for the picture and it still looked empty. The books were my wife's and mine from school. I couldn't over-extend myself financially right off the bat to buy books from publishers at retail prices. I had to be savvy, be a good buyer of my inventory from the very start.

I only had $45,000, including all loan, credit card, and personal money. So I followed the outline of my "En-trepreneur's Bible" and waited to buy textbooks at a discount from students at the end of the semester. It was definitely one of the cheaper ways to buy. I followed the textbook buyback up with sup-plementing my inven-tory with Amazon and other online purchases.

When the next semester came around, I had lots of books, but still couldn't supply the entire stu-dent body's textbook de-mands. I couldn't be all things to all people. That first semester I turned away $150,000 in lost revenue simply because I didn't have the books on

RICK·I·PEDIA
The Business Encyclopedia

Go-To-Market Strategy

Your business strategy that answers 5 questions...

1. Who is your customer?

2. What is your product?

3. What is your pricing structure?

4. What is your market plan?

5. Where will you market and sell?

the shelves to sell. Being my normal overly optimistic self, I was mildly OK with that. Remember, I knew I didn't want to get in over my head financially in the startup stage of the business. I was trying to be conservative.

True or Farse?

The Ritz cracker was introduced to markets in 1934, but we had to wait until 1953 for the invention of cheese in a can.

I had to accept the reality that I didn't have the financial ability to supply all the people with all the books they wanted, let alone the t-shirts, notebooks, calculators, backpacks, highlighters, or laptops most college bookstores upsell to students. Most importantly, my business plan didn't require me to grow my inventory in that way. I had planned to serve only a part of the textbook demand starting out, selling only USED books, while directing people who needed NEW editions to the campus store for purchase. I stayed true to my plan.

That's one of the hardest things to do as new business, to trust the research you gathered prior to opening. It was the right move to stay financially cautious and not

SENSEI SAYS

An enterprise, exist alone it cannot. Great service it can be to others. To fail at this, cease to exist it will.
— Calvin Coolidge

overextend in the infancy of my first entrepreneurial endeavor. However, when I saw the sales numbers the following month, I vowed to continue to expand my inventory to limit the amount of lost sales that walked out my door. The following semester I was in better financial shape, so I quickly expanded my inventory to include new textbooks, custom textbooks, and larger quantities of common titles. I did all I could do to increase the dollar amount of the average sale per customer. And guess what—it worked.

I recently evaluated my annual growth percentage over the first five years of my business and I was blown away. The growth rates were 50%-80% per year! The following four years have seen an average growth rate of 30% annually. I'm now in my fourth location and going stronger than ever. I had followed my "Entrepreneur's Bible" through the initial 5-year financial plan, and met every single projection! Honestly, I couldn't believe it. We had stayed focused on our customers and our go-to-market strategy and things had worked out. My caution had paid off, and my conservative projections had been realized just like I'd planned. Looking back, I can't tell you I wouldn't have changed anything, but I can preach the importance of being cautious with your spending, and the benefits of staying true to your own "Entrepreneur's Bible."

Proverb # 49

The average millionaire goes out of business twice in his lifetime. Sometimes it's harder to keep your money than make it.

've read many books depicting the lives of entrepreneurial millionaires, and it seems there is a consistent thread among many of these financially successful people. Oddly enough, most of them have horror stories of building corporations and generating great wealth only to fall quickly into bankruptcy and ruin. I looked for a key to understanding why these massive failures had occurred so often to so many hardworking people. I didn't see ties to any certain industry, age correlation, family background, education level, gender, race, or geographic location. One thing they did have in common, though. After losing all they have an average of twice in their lives, the third time these millionaires build something it finally sticks. They realize how to keep their cash cows afloat. I guess the third time's a charm.

People are always afraid of going out of business, and I can understand that fear. I have never forgotten the following sad/hilarious bankruptcy line, "I think my wife's worried about opening a store. But most businesses fail anyway, so she's not alone." Ok, yes, I laugh (inappropriately) at this line all the time, not at the trepidations we all face in putting our lives on the chopping block, when opening a new venture, but because there's an important statistic most wide-eyed young energetic entrepreneurs

RICK·I·PEDIA
The Business Encyclopedia

Exit Strategy

This is a predetermined plan that, when things go south or you chose to move on with your life, you can liquidate/sell your assets, repay your loans, and walk away from your business.

don't know about. Eighty percent of businesses fail in the first year. Wait, wait! Let it soak in. Yep, it hurts to hear that. It hurts even more to know it's true. I laugh for crying...

True or Farse?

The U.S. government keeps its supply of silver at Fort Knox.

Don't lose hope yet! Hardcore entrepreneurs have a saving grace outside of God and religion. If you further qualify that same statistic to include only people who have written an "Entrepreneur's Bible" before opening their businesses, we learn that 80% of those better prepared startups are still in business after the first year. Wait, wait! Think about it. Four out of five companies that have a specific, thought-out plan for success when they open their doors will still be in business at their one year mark.

Now, sometimes life throws you a curve ball, and for reasons unforeseen in the planning stage, your business goes south. No matter what you do, there's a chance that the market's "Invisible Hand" (see Proverb 5) will have a destructive impact on your young venture.

SENSEI SAYS

Worry no more. Do it we will.

- Richard Branson

Entrepreneurs have no choice; we have to get past our fears and realize that, as Forrest Gump observes, "life is like a box of chocolates: you never know what you're gonna get."

Don't wait around for the perfect market swing, perfect location to pop up, perfect financial situation, etc to launch a well-prepare startup. Yes, you may have to hit bottom a few times in your entrepreneurial career, like most other movers and shakers, before you realize how to keep hold of your money and stay in business. Building a long-term successful company is difficult. But after awhile it starts to be like riding a bike. You do it enough, and it becomes second nature. Soon, you'll never forget how to make money, and you'll find yourself doing entrepreneurial stunts you never thought possible!

Linda and I had a solid, thorough "Entrepreneur's Bible" when we got going, so I wasn't worried...much. Plus, we had a strong exit strategy laid out, utilizing online retailers to liquidate our products, if the worst case scenario materialized. No problem, right? Just go for it! What can happen? After a few unwanted failures you end up a millionaire with great life stories about trial and error. Sweet! At least that's how it ends in the books...(wink)

FARCE = The United States government keeps its supply of silver at the U.S. Military Academy at West Point, NY.

Proverb # 50

Tortoise vs. Hare.
The tortoise
always wins.

eing content with a slow-moving stable business is better than getting so ambitious you expand too fast and lose everything. When I hit my 2-year mark of being in business, the sales numbers looked really good. My brother came to me and asked when I was going to franchise. He wasn't the only one. I'd been asked about expanding to new locations by several others as well. People like to talk with you about growth and future markets when things are going great. When sales are down, inquirers may ask how you're going to get more customers, or simply change the subject, ignoring the business difficulty altogether. It's human nature I suppose, to avoid tough conversations.

If your business is doing well, understand that the first knee-jerk reaction people are going to throw at you is "when are you going to expand? Are you prepared to scale up?" After hearing these questions from my friends and business associates, I immediately got excited at the whole expansion proposition and looked at 60 other markets to investigate whether or not I could open other stores. Being honest with myself, I didn't feel like any of the markets met my criteria.

Unsuccessful in finding an optimal location to put a store, I went to my banker to report on the lack of expansion options. I told him that I had decided against expanding because the

RICK·I·PEDIA
The Business Encyclopedia

Franchising

The practice of using another firm's successful business model to open your own establishment.

60 cities I'd looked at didn't fit well with my store model at that time. My banker put his hand on my shoulder and told me, "you're wise beyond your years." I asked him what he meant

When Heinz launched their "green" ketchup in 2000, it delivered the highest increase in sales in the brand's history.

by that. He said, "most people expand for the sake of expanding and often damage their business in doing so. Their successful locations fund their new startups, but for unknown reasons, don't have the secret sauce of success." Trust me on this one, being successful with a stable business is way better than getting greedy, a little ambitious, expanding too fast, and costing your strong store its cash to support your new venture, often to the detriment of both.

Patience is a virtue, no matter what reality TV tells us. Don't get distracted by dollar signs, or let excitement rule your emotions. Evaluate every new location as a totally different business with its own weaknesses and threats. I want you to succeed. Don't throw it away by being too aggressive when starting out. Delay gratification. Hope that's not too "Bible" for ya.

SENSEI SAYS

How to become rich, I will tell you. Fearful you must be, when greedy others are. Greedy you must be, when fearful others become.
– Warren Buffet

Put off the quick reward today in exchange for better future gains.

For example, let's say you have had a banner year at the store and have $100,000 extra to build your business. You can try to open a new location with that cash and a new bank loan, or reinvest the money into your existing, financially successful location. When you invest in your store by taking the money you were considering spending on a risky expansion, and instead add more inventory or new product lines on the sales floor, you're delaying that "multiple store owner" title in exchange for a reasonable expectation of increased future earnings.

I faced this at my business head on when I lowered prices 11% across the board in order to increase market penetration and sales. Many of my advisors predicted that same-store revenues would drop. Wait for it...wait for it...sales actually GREW! Especially online where our prices were poised directly against our competitors'. To the surprise of my advisors our total revenue actually increased. My customers are price sensitive (who isn't), and their dollars demand that I give them what they want. By slashing prices, I obeyed the ruling will of the customer and kept my market share. It was scary, but I stayed true to this proverb and it all worked out.

TRUE

Proverb # 51

Have cash handy when hard times come-a-knockin', and they will. They'll blow your dang house down!

y business is seasonal. When my busy season sales drop off, I look to deals with wholesalers to carry me through until the next busy season comes around. Cash flow is the key during these transitions. One slow season, I had already maxed out my line of credit with the bank, and was counting on wholesale deals to bring me through the following three months. I lost my contract with my major wholesaler right as the slow season hit, and money immediately became scarce. It was scary! I had a multi-million dollar business with no cash available to pay bills for the next few months. I knew I'd have hundreds of thousands of dollars three months down the road, but on that day the well was dry. How do I get across this financial chasm without a bridge?

No problem, I thought. I had set aside emergency credit card funds totaling nearly $100,000 for cash advances, if the worst case scenario presented itself. I thought I was safe. I thought I had prepared for this day pretty well. So I went to the bank to get a cash advance and was stopped dead in my tracks. The main credit card I was depending on had a small print stipulation that only $750 could be cash advanced. A $50,000 available spending limit, but only $750 bucks approved for cash advances. That seemed ludicrous! I hadn't read the fine print on the application when I had gotten the card, thinking that all cards were created equal and just the interest rates and limits changed. I was horrified! What are these credit card companies thinking!?!

The panic attack had started, but it wouldn't

RICK·I·PEDIA
The Business Encyclopedia

Financial Chasm

Time between when revenues are depleted and future sales or capital infusions are expected.

end there. I needed about $20,000 by the next business day or we were in trouble. I tried the next card in my so far impotent arsenal. Again, my cash advance was limited to only $3,500. I flashed a third card

out on the counter. Cash advance limit held at 50% of the card's limit. That gave me about $10,000 more. Could I get through the next few days with this? I decided quickly, no. I emptied out my personal credit card cash advances, savings account, and checking account. I had enough money now to last about a month. But what about the following two months of famine before the flood of high seasonal sales? I went to my bank for a new loan, based on future sales, and got a signature loan for $25,000 within the week! "OK, so maybe, if the famine doesn't end up so bad, I might be able to make it," I thought. No such luck. Half way through the second month I ran out of money again. I needed cash. I even tried charging my credit card through my store's credit card machine, which I later found out was illegal. It didn't go through, luckily, and I'm still felony-free.

SENSEI SAYS
A time there was, when a fool and his moeny, soon parted they were. To everyone now it happens.
– Adlai E. Stevenson

I came home after exhausting every single one of my options, and looked at my wife and said, "Linda, I don't have enough money for the store. We're in the hole. I haven't slept in a month. I've done all I can.

I need thousands of dollars and I don't know where it's going to come from." She thought for a split second, turned, and bolted to the other room. She came back with her hands full of cash and said, "is $25,000 enough?" I lost my breath and smiled giddily, cash gushing out of her palm. I grabbed the money and counted it in a frenzy. Her home-based business had been a cash cow for the previous 4-5 months and I hadn't even noticed! She had been keeping this cash in her bathroom drawer waiting to deposit it in an account for the kids education fund, but had never gotten around to it. I felt absolutely no guilt for taking money from my kids' education fund. My business now had enough cash to exist. We got a new wholesaler that was nearly as good as the one we had lost, cut a few expenses, and made it to the promised land of seasonal sales.

It was a roller-coaster, but we made it through. That's your job as an entrepreneur. Stay in business. Do whatever you have to do to keeping making money and paying the bills. Solve all the problems that are thrown at you. That's your job. It's why you get paid the big bucks. And definitely don't trust credit cards to bail you out of an emergency. Always, always, always take money from lenders when you DON'T need it, because when you DO need it you won't be able to get it. I was lucky. I had a conservative wife to help me with my mania!

Proverb # 52

Before you expand, ask yourself if the extra profit will be worth the extra time and hassle.

've worked with retail, bank, and fast food cashiers in the past, and they always count down their cash drawers to the penny after every shift. In over a decade of running a retail store, I haven't counted down any of my cash drawers to the penny...EVER. We count down the dollars daily, but not the change. It takes time, and then, if the drawer is off a penny, I have to get it from my employee. Come on, it's just change. How much is more time and less stress worth to you?

I knew a construction general contractor a few years back. Let's call him Joe. Joe had a thriving business with a charismatic team leader and 10 additional hard working guys on his crew. He was putting in around 40 hours per week and making net take-home pay of $80,000 per year. Joe loved his career. He was a true craftsman, and his customers agreed. In fact, he was so well liked by his customers that he was getting multiple referrals weekly. He was having to turn away several jobs each month because his team was just too busy. He found himself turning away so much business, and passing it on to his buddies' companies, that he thought one day, "what if I built up a second team to take on these referral jobs? Maybe I'll be able to double my income!"

Joe immediately went all in. He promoted his team leader to the general contractor position

RICK·I·PEDIA
The Business Encyclopedia

Product Line

A group of related products you stock in order to upsell customers interested in one product within the group.

over the main crew, and hired 10 guys for a new second team that he would personally manage. As we all know, when you pursue a new endeavor, you're adding more hours

Painting a house yellow or having a yellow trim hurts its value and makes it sell more slowly.

to your day, filled with additional paperwork, random responsibility, and employee issues. Joe ended up increasing his weekly work load from the comfortable 40 hours per week to around 70 hours. While he was training his new team and managing their projects, he found himself having to spend a lot of time overseeing his original crew and coaching his old team leader into that general contractor role. To top it all off, customer complaints were increasing, a problem he'd never faced in all his years of construction.

At the end of the year, Joe looked at his net take-home pay. It had gone up with the new crew, but only to about $110,000. He sat down and thought about the pay increase. It wasn't proportional to the hours he was working, not to mention the fact that his body couldn't continue working this many hours much longer. He ended up dropping his new team after that first year and went back to leading his original team, working 40 hours a week, and making his $80,000. Guess what. He was happy.

Often in business we find major opportunities for growth and expansion, but know that there's a lot more to expanding than just making more money. No matter what, you're gonna have customer satisfaction and complaints, inventory management, additional silos of communication and authority, new facility and equipment costs, management of new employees, etc. Sometimes it's work, work, work, with less than the expected reward. Make sure bigger is going to be better...(wink)

In my industry, college bookstores, most of my competitors have several income streams from multiple product lines beyond just textbooks, like backpacks, calculators, highlighters, even doilies! When evaluating what to carry, I researched how my gross margin percentages would change in my little store if I added any of these additional product lines. My projections came out grim. I thought beyond the initial product costs to all the new facility and utility costs, inventory control systems, new employees, display costs, insurance and maintenance fees, and computer needs I'd face if I started carrying more goods. After all the additional work and expenses, my numbers showed that net profit was only going to be boosted by around 10%.

The sales just weren't projected to justify the expansion. I felt that if I added the product lines, I'd end up like that general contractor trying to boost revenue, but working twice as hard for only a little more money. Needless to say, I didn't expand at that time, and was much happier because

SENSEI SAYS
Make meaning. The best reason to start an organization, it is. When create you do a product or service, hoping to make the world, you are.
- Guy Kawasaki

of it. Yes, I didn't grab every last penny from my customers with impulse purchases. But it's not always about the money. Once you're beyond Maslow's first couple of rungs in his hierarchy of needs (see Proverb 38), a whole world of incentives become apparent to you, most of which are not monetary based.

BE WARNED! Money talks, and it can call to all of us. We have to decide if our time is worth the extra cash. Once we're engaged in an expansion, it's hard to withdraw. Believe me, money isn't everything, as this general contractor realized. Life is worth more than the cash it takes to sustain it.

FARCE = Painting a house yellow or having a yellow trim helps a house sell faster.

CONCLUSION

Recall back to the introduction of this book where I asked you to take the Duree Diamond Entrepreneurship Personality Test and honestly judge yourself. You were to make a dot on the Diamond where your answers to the questions had you land. Now that you've devoured these 52 Proverbs of Profit, flip to the introduction in the front of the book and take the personality test again. Make a new dot on the Diamond. Where do you find yourself now? Have you moved to the right at all? Are you ready for more risk and reward in your life? Or perhaps you've discovered that heading out on your own isn't in the cards for you. If that's the case, I'm glad I could help you save the money you may have lost in opening a business. Hey, entrepreneurship isn't for everyone. But one thing's for sure: once an entrepreneur, always an entrepreneur.

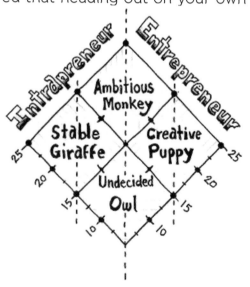

I hope you enjoyed these 52 Proverbs of Profit. Thanks for paying it forward by sharing all the entrepreneurial secrets you've found in this book online with your friends on Facebook and LinkedIn. Thanks for reading, and God Bless!

Original
SENSEI SAYS QUOTES

Proverb 1
If you don't drive your business, you will be driven out
of business.
- B. C. Forbes

Proverb 2
The majority of men meet with failure because of
their lack of persistence in creating new plans to take
the place of those which fail.
- Napoleon Hill

Proverb 3
To turn really interesting ideas and fledgling
technologies into a company that can continue to
innovate for years, it requires a lot of disciplines.
- Steve Jobs

Proverb 4
Without continual growth and progress, such words
as improvement, achievement, and success have no
meaning.
- Benjamin Franklin

Proverb 5
Far and away the best prize that life offers is the
chance to work hard at work worth doing.
- Theodore Roosevelt

Proverb 6
If you owe the bank $100 that's your problem. If you
owe the bank $100 million, that's the bank's problem.
- J. Paul Getty

Proverb 7
Big pay and little responsibility are circumstances
seldom found together.
- Napoleon Hill

Proverb 8
The man who will use his skill and constructive
imagination to see how much he can give for a dollar,
instead of how little he can give for a dollar, is bound
to succeed.
- Henry Ford

Proverb 9
Too many of us are not living our dreams because we
are living our fears.
- Les Brown

Proverb 10
In the business world, everyone is paid in two coins:
cash and experience. Take the experience first; the
cash will come later.
- Harold S. Geneen

Proverb 11
Identify your problems but give your power and
energy to solutions.
- Tony Robbins

Proverb 12
Profit in business comes from repeat customers,
customers that boast about your project or service,
and that bring friends with them.
- W. Edwards Deming

Proverb 13
Willingness to change is a strength, even if it means plunging part of the company into total confusion for a while.
– Jack Welch

Proverb 14
Management is nothing more than motivating other people.
– Le Iacocca

Proverb 15
Opportunity is missed by most people because it is dressed in overalls and looks like work.
– Thomas Edison

Proverb 16
Business is a combination of war and sport.
– Andre Maurois

Proverb 17
The more you lose yourself in something bigger than yourself, the more energy you will have.
– Norman Vincent Peale

Proverb 18
Innovation distinguishes between a leader and a follower.
– Steve Jobs

Proverb 19
The financial markets generally are unpredictable.
So that one has to have different scenarios. The idea
that you can actually predict what's going to happen
contradicts my way of looking at the market.
- George Soros

Proverb 20
You only have to do a very few things right in your life
so long as you don't do too many things wrong.
- Warren Buffett

Proverb 21
An economist is an expert who will know tomorrow
why the things he predicted yesterday didn't happen
today.
- Laurence J. Peter

Proverb 22
It is not the strongest of the species that survive, nor
the most intelligent, but the one most responsive to
change.
- Charles Darwin

Proverb 23
The first responsibility of a leader is to define reality.
The last is to say thank you. In between, the leader is
a servant.
- Max dePree

Proverb 25
It's not your salary that makes you rich, it's your
spending habits.
- Charles A. Jaffe

Proverb 26
One of the hardest things you can do in business is create demand.
- Jim Elder

Proverb 27
The absolute fundamental aim is to make money out of satisfying customers.
- John Egan

Proverb 28
Most people struggle with life balance simply because they haven't paid the price to decide what is really important to them.
- Stephen Covey

Proverb 29
Effort only fully releases its reward after a person refuses to quit.
- Napoleon Hill

Proverb 30
Whenever you find yourself on the side of the majority, it is time to pause and reflect.
- Mark Twain

Proverb 32
Nearly all men can stand adversity, but if you want to test a man's character, give him power.
- Abraham Lincoln

Proverb 33
You are educated. Your certification is in your degree.
You may think of it as the ticket to the good life. Let
me ask you to think of an alternative. Think of it as
your ticket to change the world.
- Tom Brokaw

Proverb 34
Hire character. Train skill.
- Peter Schutz

Proverb 35
I find that when you have a real interest in life and a
curious life, that sleep is not the most important thing.
- Martha Stewart

Proverb 36
Motivation is the art of getting people to do what you
want them to do because they want to do it.
- Dwight D. Eisenhower

Proverb 37
Why did I want to win? Because I didn't want to lose!
- Max Schmelling

Proverb 38
To succeed... You need to find something to hold on
to, something to motivate you, something to inspire
you.
- Tony Dorsett

Proverb 39
The entrepreneur always searches for change,
responds to it, and exploits it as an opportunity.
- Peter F. Drucker

Proverb 40
The most serious mistakes are not being made as a result of wrong answers. The truly dangerous thing is asking the wrong question.
–Peter F. Drucker

Proverb 41
Government in the U.S. today is a senior partner in every business in the country.
- Norman Cousins

Proverb 42
In business, I've discovered that my purpose is to do my best to my utmost ability every day. That's my standard. I learned early in my life that I had high standards.
- Donald Trump

Proverb 43
The invisible hand of the market always moves faster and better than the heavy hand of government.
- Mitt Romney

Proverb 44
A business has to be involving, it has to be fun, and it has to exercise your creative instincts.
- Richard Branson

Proverb 45
Remind people that profit is the difference between revenue and expense. This makes you look smart.
- Scott Adams

Proverb 46
We've got to do everything we can to make entrepreneurial dreams a reality. - Ross Perot

Proverb 47
Capital isn't scarce; vision is.
- Sam Walton

Proverb 48
No enterprise can exist for itself alone. It ministers to some great need, it performs some great service, not for itself, but for others, or failing therein, it ceases to be profitable and ceases to exist.
- Calvin Coolidge

Proverb 49:
rew it, Let's do it!
Richard Branson

roverb 50
I will tell you how to become rich. Close the doors. Be fearful when others are greedy. Be greedy when others are fearful.
- Warren Buffett

Proverb 51
There was a time when a fool and his money were soon parted, but now it happens to everybody.
- Adlai E. Stevenson

Proverb 52
The best reason to start an organization is to make meaning; to create a product or service to make the world a better place.
- Guy Kawasaki